C000089775

King Arthur in Irish

Pseudo-Historical

Tradition

An Introduction

DANE PESTANO

© 2011 Dane Pestano. Historian, Sussex UK.

All rights reserved. Except as permitted under current legislation no part of this work may be photocopied, stored in a retrieval system, published, performed in public, adapted, broadcast, transmitted, recorded or reproduced in any form or by any means, without prior permission of the copyright owner.

First published by

Dark Age Arthurian Books

2011

ISBN 978-0-9570002-0-9

This small work is dedicated to all those brilliant scholars who have done so much work in the past to make this work a possibility and to the invention of the internet which has made research available to one and all. Special thanks also go out to those contributors of the *Arthurian Myths and Legends, Old Irish L* and *Arthurnet* online discussion groups who have been very helpful.

Contents

Preface

The story of Arthur

The great King Arthur, defeater of Saxons, Picts and Scots, conqueror of Britain, Ireland, Scotland, Denmark, Gaul and the Orkneys needs no introduction being probably the most famous ancient Briton of all time, but as we will be comparing his life with that of certain Irish legends a brief summary of what is known of his life and their sources would be useful.

Arthur first appears through the mists of time in the early ninth century work the *Historia Brittonum* (HB) – the History of the Britons - composed around 829AD[1]. This work was an accumulation of various sources bundled together and rewritten to form a whole narrative history. The work incorporates material concerning a chronology of ancient British events; material on Vortigern[2], Ambrosius Aurelianus[3], St.Germanus[4] and St.Patrick[5] , Arthur's battles, Northern British events, the mirablilia[6] and Saxon genealogies.

---

[1] Dumville, David N. Histories and Pseudo-histories of the Insular Middle Ages, Variorum, Gower Publishing Group 1990.

[2] The king who invited the Saxons to Britain as mercenaries against the Picts and Scots(Irish)

[3] The last of the Romans according to Gildas, who organised British defenses in the fifth century and brought victory to the Britons over the Saxons.

[4] A Bishop sent to Britain from Gaul two times (429 and again later) to quell heretical Christian beliefs.

[5] A Briton who went to Northern Ireland of his own volition in around 456 to convert the heathen Irish and was eventually made a Bishop in old age and died circa 493.

In this work then, Arthur's twelve battles[7] are mentioned for the first time, where he is said to have defeated the Anglo Saxons and won every battle including the famous battle of Badon hill. We also get a glimpse of the mythology that has begun to surround him as he became associated with the landscape due to the similarity of his name to various rock formations. Therefore, he is associated with a Neolithic tomb in Ercing in Wales and to another stone associated with a giant mythical dog of his called Cabal[8].

In the HB Arthur is merely called in Latin a *dux bellorum* or *miles*, the former meaning a 'general or leader of battle' and the latter a 'soldier' or 'mounted warrior'. From this, it has been deduced that he may have been of lower rank than the kings of the Britons he fought for, but this may not be the case. Medieval scribes in copying ancient manuscripts often changed the title of *Rex* (king) to that of *Dux* (General) or *Comes* (Count) as they didn't recognise the status of the petty king. This was due to the time in which they wrote, not understanding that in the fifth and sixth centuries the whole country would have been full of petty kings and their kingdoms, with several kings occupying small areas that were later amalgamated under one sovereignty. The

---

[6] Mythology linked to landscape and nature features.

[7] The first at the mouth of the river Glein, the second, third, fourth and fifth were on another river called Dubglas in the region of Linnuis, the sixth on the river Bassus, the seventh in the Caledonian forest, the eighth at Guinnion fort, the ninth in the city of the Legion, the tenth on the river called Tribruit, the eleventh on the hill called Agned, and the twelfth was on Badon Hill and it nine hundred and sixty men fell in one day from a single assault by Arthur, and no one lay them low save he alone.

[8] Meaning 'horse'. i.e. a giant dog.

poetic epithet of *dux bellorum* (leader of battles) itself was a common enough one in Welsh poetry, suggesting, as many scholars have done, that the Arthur battle list derived from a Welsh poem of the seventh or eighth centuries. The HB was appended to over many years, with some more information on Arthur included, such as glosses to the main work. These made more of his Christian links and offered some puzzling comments concerning his wayward youth. The Irish then wrote their own vernacular version of the HB in the mid eleventh century[9].

The next we hear of Arthur is in the tenth century poem *The Gododdin*[10]. This poem concerning events of Britons living in what is now southern Scotland around Edinburgh compared one of their heroes Gwawrddur to Arthur, implying that he was not as great as Arthur even though he could kill 300 men[11]. This comparison is based on the battle list in the HB as Arthur was said to be able to kill 960 men in one assault[12]. The poem also shows many more borrowings from the HB so can be dated in its Arthurian form sometime after the HB became widely read. Therefore, for this part a tenth century date seems appropriate even though the manuscript we have now only dates from the

---

[9] See main thesis below for full details.

[10] Willis, David. Old and Middle Welsh in The Celtic languages, edited by Martin Ball and Nicole Müller. London: Routledge, 117-60. He refers to the poem as old Welsh. (850-1150). The earliest MS is C13th but Isaac, Dumville, Higham and others date it to the C10th or C11th based on the orthography. Whether it was orally transmitted from the C7th is unknown.

[11] He fed black ravens on the rampart of a fortress, though he was no Arthur.

[12] See Higham, N.J. King Arthur, Myth Making and History, Routledge, 2002 who discusses these issues.

thirteenth century. The poem refers to a battle that took place in Scotland in the late sixth century called Catraeth, which is mentioned in the Irish annals as having taken place in 596AD[13] against Saxons incursions into far northern Britain. Also in the tenth century, we find Arthur mentioned in the Welsh Annals as having fought at Badon in the year 516 and having died in 537 in battle, at the same time as one Medraut (Mordred) but it is possible these are later interpolations to the annals.

Arthur then reappears next in an early eleventh century text called *Vita Goeznovius* (circa 1016) which has taken material from a continental version of the HB, which detailed his twelve battles against the Saxons and then mentions for the first time his conquest of Gaul and his kingship[14].

In around 1120 a Flemish cleric called Lambert of St Omer, in a work entitled *Liber Floridus* mentions a palace of Arthur situated in Pictland, *"built with marvelous art and variety, in which the history of all his exploits and wars are to be seen in sculpture"*. These sculptures are most likely those at the Pictish capital Forteviot as opposed to the medieval belief that Arthurs Oven near the river Carron is meant. Soon after this in 1125, William of Malmesbury in the *Gesta Regum Anglorum* mentions

---

[13] 'Bellum Ratho in Druad' Annals of Ulster.

[14] "[The Saxons'] arrogance was presently, as occasion presented itself, repressed then by great Arthur king of the Britons, so that they were driven out of most of the island and forced to serve. But when that same Arthur, after many victories which he accomplished illustriously in British and Gaulish areas, finally called from human endeavor, [the island] was again forcibly exposed to the Saxons. Ashe, Geoffrey. The Legend of St. Goeznovius, (1991). "Legenda Sancti Goeznovii". Also see Lacy, Norris J. The New Arthurian Encyclopedia, pp. 204–205, Garland, 1991.

Arthur where he says that Arthur was the subject of *"fantastic tales told by the Bretons"*.[15] This is then followed by the most famous or infamous work to mention Arthur, the *History of the Kings of Britain* written by Geoffrey of Monmouth in about 1139. This expands on the legends of Arthur and Geoffrey uses him as a figurehead to appease the British and English who had recently been conquered by the Normans with Breton help. He does this by linking Arthur to Breton descent and envisages the Bretons playing a major role in the conquest of the Saxons as they did in helping the Normans of William the Conqueror defeat Harold.

Also in this century are other works from the Welsh such as *Culhwch and Olwen* and other fairy tales that mention Arthur from a group of works now called *the Mabinogian.* It was Geoffrey's work though which was to inspire the later romance tales of Arthur, including as it does mention of Merlin and Mordred and others that became linked with Arthurian legend. It is in this work that Arthur was given a father 'Uther'[16], whose deeds are merely a mirror of Arthur's. It is here we find his wife for the first time, Guinevere, his famous sword Caliburnus, later Excalibur, his extended battles against the Saxons (in various places Geoffrey assumes they took place) an expanded version of Arthur's conquest of Gaul, southern Scotland and Ireland, his non

---

[15] Loomis, R.S. Scotland and the Arthurian Legend. Columbia University. Proceedings of the Society 1955/56.

[16] Meaning the 'horrible or terrible one'.

death as he sails away to Avalon to heal his wounds and much more.

From here on in Geoffrey's work found its way to the continent and the French Romance writers picked up the story and incorporated their own localised legends of Arthur mixed with Greek mythology to create a chivalric Arthur and his knights, born to uphold late medieval moral values and take part in the search for the Holy Grail. Other later writers then incorporated the Round Table to accommodate Arthurs many knights in equal sitting and the legend of Arthur was complete.

Arthur then, after the death of Uther , as a lad of fifteen, was chosen to lead the Britons after pulling a sword from a stone, signifying his right to rule. He moved against the Saxons, Irish and Picts fighting twelve battles with the help of his Breton allies culminating in the great battle of Badon where the Saxons were finally defeated and peace brought to Britain. He is given Excalibur from the Lady of the Lake to help in his wars. He was then threatened by the king of Gaul who called for the Britons to give tribute to the Romans as they had done in the past. This Arthur refused and set out to conquer Gaul instead, as many Romano British emperors had done in the past. He was successful in this and then married Guinevere and thought all was well but in a second campaign to Gaul he left his foster son Mordred in control of Britain. Mordred wanted the crown for himself so traitorously enrolled the help of the Saxons to usurp power. At this Arthur returned from his campaigns and fought against Mordred, which culminated in the great battle of Camlann in 537[17] where Arthur killed Mordred; but Arthur, mortally wounded, was carried off to the isle of Avalon. Arthur was now said to sleep in a cave waiting to return to save the Britons once more in their hour of need. Unfortunately, to stop this idea that the Britons had for salvation from the Norman conquest, the Norman King of England decided to orchestrate the finding of 'Arthurs' bones buried under Glastonbury Tor, complete with fake inscription. Arthur was now never to return but this did not stop his legends growing to even greater heights over the centuries.

The biggest question for those seeking Arthur now is did he actually exist? From a scholarly viewpoint the evidence is scant to say the least, his name[18] a puzzle to etymologists and contemporary evidence for his very existence is missing. Many have sought to find the original Arthur on whom these legends have grown but no one has been able to place their person in the right time frame. Instead we have the Roman - Lucius Artorius Castus from the second century AD who actually fought against the Britons as a suggestion[19]; or Riothamus a fifth century British leader who fought in 470AD against the Goths in Gaul and lost[20];

---

[17] From the tenth century Welsh Annals. Geoffrey of Monmouth made the date 545 for reasons best known to himself.

[18] In various sources as Arthur, Artus, Arcturus, Arturius, Arturus and Artuir.

[19] Littleton, C. Scott, Malcor, Linda, From Scythia to Camelot: A Radical Reassessment of the Legends of King Arthur, the Knights of the Round Table and the Holy Grail, New York, Garland, 2000

or Artuir Mac Aedan[21] an insignificant Arthur of Irish descent who died in the late sixth or early seventh century, as well as others such as Arthur Ap Pedr, again of the seventh century.

What no one has been able to do is find legends concerning an Arthur like person that fits him into his correct time frame of the late fifth to the mid sixth century; that has him fight the Saxons, Irish and Picts and assume power over them all including the Danes and the Orkneys. That has him conquer the Gauls twice, has a wife Guinevere, has him raised by a druid, has special weapons and is not initially a king of the Britons. Not only this, but no one has been able to link such a person to an historical king living in the sixth century whose name could represent the name Arthur. What this current work sets out to do is present exactly those requirements in the form of annals and legends hidden for hundreds of years, some still awaiting translation. This material is brand new to the subject of Arthuriana and has never been presented before. This work therefore is an introduction to Arthuriana of this fascinating and rather brutal character of Irish history, pseudo-history and mythology. I will start first with an introduction to the character and to the sources in which he appears. I will then discuss his name, family and background and then move onto his battles. After this the main story of his life and deeds will then be presented as a narrative work.

---

[20] Ashe, Geoffrey. "A Certain Very Ancient Book: Traces of an Arthurian Source in Geoffrey of Monmouth's History", *Speculum*. 1981

Introduction.

As late as 1999 Ceridwen Lloyd-Morgan, author of '*The Celtic Tradition*' when summarising the paucity of Irish material concerning King Arthur wrote "*it is clear that there was no early, indigenous, Irish Arthurian tradition*" and "*Arthurian material in Irish is rare, late and derivative.*"[22] Then in 2004 Ann Dooley in the introduction to her paper, *Arthur Of the Irish: A Viable Concept?* wrote these words:

"*Arthur never figured in medieval Irish tradition in any significant way; indeed, it is precisely because whatever traces may be recovered of an Arthurian tradition in Ireland are presumed to carry for an Irish scene none of the same configurations, developments and cultural concerns as in Britain, that these Arthurian markers have never seriously been revised or considered. For reasons that are as much political as historical, Arthur is only of minor interest to Irish scholars and a study of Arthuriana will be presumed to yield no insights for the course of Ireland's own distinctive cultural or political history.*"[23]

---

[21] For an essay on the problems of this Artuir see Zeigler, Michelle, Artur Mac Aedan of Dalriada, Heroic Age, Issue 1, Spring/Summer 1999. http://www.mun.ca/mst/heroicage/issues/1/haaad.htm

[22] Barron, W. R. J. ed., The Arthur of the English: The Arthurian Legend in Medieval English Life and Literature, University of Wales Press, 1999. She points out the earliest reference to Arthur in Irish material is by Fionn O Dalaigh who died in 1387.

[23] Lloyd-Morgan, C. Ed., Arthurian Literature XXI: Celtic Arthurian Material: Celtic Arthurian Material v. 21 2004.

12

Ann then goes on to detail many associations between Arthurian legends with those of Irish works and her paper is a great introduction to the Irish Arthurian subject. This lack of interest and lack of evidence for an Irish Arthur has been the received opinion of scholars for generations, long before Lloyd-Morgan and following.

The Dal Riadic Artuir Mac Aedan is the closest anyone has come to an Irish source for Arthur and was most recently suggested by Maney (2004)[24] who pointed out that the source of the Historia Brittonum battle list of Arthur may have had a Strathclyde origin. Most commentators though dismiss Artuir as the origin for the stories of Arthur as he was such an insignificant character and his father Aedan, a famous warrior of the time, would surely have entered Arthurian lore. The time period is also wrong for Artuir who exists in the late sixth century, a time at which recordable history was verifiable and hence there would have been little doubt about him. Lastly, the Irish annals show that Artuir's entry in them was added much later using the late seventh century *Life of St Columba* by Adamnan as a source and hence the note of his death is unreliable.

More recently in 2007 Tom Green in *Concepts of Arthur*[25] has no conception of an Irish Arthurian figure beyond comparing the Arthur legend with that of the mythical Irish hero Finn or Fionn.

---

[24] Maney Laurence J, Looking For Arthur In All The Wrong Places, Proceedings of The Harvard Celtic Colloquium 2004/2005.

[25] Tempus Publishing, 2007. An excellent summary of Arthurian study and theories.

He suggests that the Arthurian legend came about in a similar way to that of the legends of Finn in Ireland. This may indeed hold some truth, but overlooks the fact that the Irish did know of an 'Arthur' and had their own traditions and legends concerning him. However, they called him by a name completely different to what anyone would expect. For this reason the Irish Arthur has lain hidden; his legends scattered throughout Irish manuscripts, waiting for the pieces to fall into place and the story of this forgotten 'Irish' hero revealed and told again for the first time in hundreds of years. Not only do the Irish have legends about an Arthur figure, but also, contrary to the Welsh material, the Irish actually link him to a confirmed historical sixth century king! Even more astounding than this is that his descendants through his sons' daughter become kings of Saxon Northumbria in the seventh century!

It is generally known that pseudo-historical works such as the ninth century *Historia Brittonum* (HB) and the *Welsh Annals* owe a great deal too Irish influence in their conception and construction[26]. The fact that there is so much Irish influence on such works has been frustrating for those seeking a reason as to why Arthur is not present or features very rarely in early Irish literature, especially from the ninth century when the HB coagulated some Arthurian legend into its pages and would have been well read in Ireland. In fact by the eleventh century, the

[26] Dumville, David. Histories and Pseudo-Histories of the Insular Middle Ages. Variorum, Gower Publishing Group, 1990 and St Patrick A.D. 493-1993 Dumville et al, Boydell Press 1993.

Irish had written their own version of the HB and called it the Lebhor Bretnach - '*The Book of the Bretons or Britons*'. In this collection of manuscripts was a legend, so weird and so outlandish[27], that it was relegated to the appendix when the Irish HB was examined and published by Todd and Herbert in 1848[28]. This tale of St Cairnech once occupied a place in the Ballymote version of the Irish HB detailing events from an Irish perspective following Roman withdrawal from Britain to the mid sixth century. It was and still is relegated to a mere appendix and hence became 'lost' to readers of the Irish HB and its significance forgotten. It was in this discarded tale that the key to finding the Irish Arthur lay. In these tales St.Cairnech is identical to the British St.Carannog or Carantoc, both having the same feast day of May 16th. Carantoc, in his Vita, is one of the few saints to be associated with King Arthur.

Ann Dooley's study of the story of St Cairnech suggests that it is possible that this tale was originally part of the Irish HB compiled by Gilla Coemain[29] in the mid eleventh century, although it is not certain that he wrote the story itself[30]. Dooley suggests that an eleventh century date would fit in with the local politics of Brega and Tethba in Ireland of the time.[31] As this

---

[27] 'Of The Miracles of Cairnech Here'.

[28] Todd, J.H. and Herbert, A. The Irish Version Of The Historia Brittonum of Nennius', Irish Archaeological Society Dublin, Dublin, 1848.

[29] Died circa 1072

[30] Ibid Dooley Pg. 12

[31] Ibid Dooley Pg. 12

current work is an introduction though, I will not expand on the political, social and historical events of the ninth to eleventh centuries that may have influenced these tales or delve into the many possibilities these tales engender apart from some footnote suggestions. Dooley did know of this Irish hero and described his story in her work but did not take the idea to its more obvious conclusion.

I have spent the good part of four years researching these legends and this has lead to perhaps the greatest question and answer of all; who was King Arthur? In a larger work I will expand on this research and come to conclusions concerning the historical man himself, but for now enjoy the forgotten story of the Irish Arthur in all his violent glory, at the correct time in history and in all the right places.........

Muircertach Mac Erca

"And then the power and strength of Britain was destroyed after him"

Muircertach Mac Erca, as Irish legend tells us, was a High king of Ireland, son of Muiredach, son of Eoghan, son of Niall of the Nine Hostages. Reputedly, he was the first Christian King of Ireland[32] who reigned from around 510[33] or 513[34] until about 534 or 537[35]. He fought numerous battles, was in his early years a murderous tyrant, exacted tribute, was in possession of the Lia Fáil, conquered Ireland and Gaul and assumed the sovereignty of Britain, Scotland, the Saxons, Denmark and the Orkneys; is fostered by a Druid and is finally given the ultimate accolade of a famous hero – the triple death. If this set of circumstances sounds familiar you would be right; this is the same as King Arthur was supposed to have accomplished as related by Nennius and Geoffrey of Monmouth and exactly during the same time period!

---

[32] His Christian leaning is suggested by the lack of a Feiss Temro (a pagan kingship and marriage ceremony), during his reign. See Carney, James. 'Studies in Irish Literature and History' Dublin Institute for Advanced Studies, 1955 p. 338. See also Smith, P. J. Imarcaigh sund ar gach saí : An Early Modern Irish Poem on the Contemporaneous Emperors of Byzantium and the Kings and Ecclesiastics of Ireland, , University of Ulster, Poem twelfth to fifteenth century in which Muircertach is mentioned : *"The death of Muircheartach son of Earc about that time – he was no heathen".*

[33] Annals of Tigernach

[34] Annals of Ulster

[35] The Alternative dates occur in myth and the Irish Annals. He reigned for 24 years and in Aided MM Erca 25 years. From the AU 513 this would give 537. Note Arthur is supposed to have died in 537, according to the Welsh Annals of the tenth century or later.

Muircertach's story is told in various existing ancient Irish manuscripts. The fourteenth century *Yellow Book of Lecan*, the sixth to twelfth century *Irish Annals*, the eleventh to twelfth century *Dinshenchas* and *Banshenchus*, tenth to twelfth century *Book of Leinster* and *Laud Synchronisms*, the twelfth century *Banquet of Dun Na nGedh* and the fourteenth century *Book of Ballymote* which includes the *Lebor Bretnach* or 'Book of the Britons'. Most of these books were compiled using earlier sources and hence the provenance of the stories has a more ancient origin. Muircertach was also mentioned in a now lost work called *Echtra Muircheartach Mac Erca* – The Navigation or Journeys of Muircheartach Mac Erca[36], mentioned in the *Book of Leinster* which may have told the story of his Gallic campaign. Cendfaeladh, a seventh century poet and possible descendent of Mac Erca is attributed with various verses recording his exploits[37]. His mythical death is mention in the tale called *Aided Muircertach Mac Erca* – The Violent Death of Muircertach Mac Erca (referred to as Aided from now on).

---

[36] Another variation existed called Immram Luinge Murchertaig –'*Voyage of the Ship of Muircertach son of Erc'*. Moylan, Tom, Irish Voyages and Visions: Pre-Figuring, Re-configuring Utopia, Utopian Studies 18.3, 2007.

[37] Irish and Scottish Annals.

The Lebhor Bretnach
Of The Miracles of Cairnech Here.

The *Lebhor Bretnach* is the Irish version of the *Historia Brittonum* compiled in the eleventh century where Muircertach's story forms part of the tale: *Of the Miracles of Cairnech Here.* This story of St. Cairnech, Mac Erca and Lugaide appears to be of eleventh to fourteenth century hagiographical origin derived from an earlier lost life of St Cairnech compiled with other earlier material on Mac Erca that has been added to the Ballymote version of the *Lebhor Bretnach* and placed into the chronology of that work after the year 422 when the Romans had left Britain. Therefore, it was intended to cover the period from the Roman withdrawal to the mid sixth century[38]. The earlier date for some of the material stems from the fact that the slaying of Lugaide by Mac Erca is mentioned in the *Baile Chuin* MS of the seventh to ninth centuries – *"Fierce Lugaid of noble great drinking shall be approached: ordeal of battle. A glorious man upon him, Mac Ercéne."* The details about Mac Erca's triumphs may have come from the lost story of his journeys as described above.

The story of St Cairnech appears to be a composition utilising various sources. The first being genealogical, possibly of the tenth century, explaining the ancestry of the various characters, the second an earlier source detailing some of Mac Erca's

---

[38] ibid Todd, Herbert, Dublin, 1848. Pg.xiii

adventures and the third being material about St Cairnech himself. It is an interesting tale that does not appear to know of Muircertach's connection with the fairy woman Sheen or of his mythical death at Cleitech, suggesting some essence of the tale may have pre-dated the later myth making of the tenth century onwards. It would seem inconceivable that a writer of a Vita about St. Cairnech would leave out the story of his involvement with Mac Erca's death had it been known. In this story, Mac Erca's sin is that he has taken the wife of Lugaide, whom he had defeated earlier, whereas in the story of his death his sin is that he takes on the concubine Sheen and throws out his wife Duinsech. In this story there is no mention of the Danes or Vikings, instead it features the Franks, Britons, Picts, Irish and Saxons suggesting an early date for the parts about Mac Erca, possibly late eighth to early ninth century.

In their 1848 publication of the *Irish version of the Historia Brittonum*, Todd and Herbert suggested this tale must be later than the year 1079 as this was when Pope Gregory the VII officially granted the primacy of the See of Lyons in writing. In the story, Cairnech makes a pilgrimage possibly to Lyon[39]. However in reading Gregory's letter confirming the primacy he states that it was already seen as such and also decreed by those who came before him:

---

[39] The place is named as 'Lien' in the story, so the identity of the place is still debatable.

"....by its appointment and authority, the church of Lyons is acknowledged for long to have held the primacy over the four provinces of Lyons, Rouen, Tours and Sens. Therefore we...wishing to follow the examples of the holy fathers and relying on their power, desire at due time to confirm the primacy of Lyons that they established and sanctioned by their decrees"[40]

It is clear then that Lyons was considered the primary see of the area long before 1079, even if it was on pseudo decretals of the ninth century that Gregory based his decision[41]. Therefore, some of this story of St Cairnech could indeed date from the ninth century and some of its sources to as early as the seventh.

---

[40] James E. - Luscombe David E. - McKitterick, Rosamond. - Reuter, Timothy The new Cambridge medieval history. - Cambridge University Press – 2006, pg.234.

[41] He may have used the false Decretal of Anecletus. See Delivre, Fabrice. The Foundations of Primatial Claims in the Western Church (Eleventh–Thirteenth Centuries). The Journal of Ecclesiastical History, 2008. 59, pp 383-406.

The Yellow Book of Lecan

Aided Muircertach Mac Erca.

The Yellow book of Lecan (*Leabhar Buidhe Lecain*) in which the Story of Mac Erca's death - *Aided Muircertach Mac Erca*[42] (*The violent death of Muircertach Mac Erca*) appears is a Middle Irish composition amalgamated in the fifteenth century from manuscripts of the fourteenth and fifteenth centuries. These in turn were based on older manuscripts. The *Yellow Book of Lecan* contains many stories of Irish mythology, including nearly all of the Ulster cycle series of legends.

Aided Muircertach Mac Erca is likely a composition of the tenth to eleventh centuries using various sources for some of the details of Mac Erca's exploits; perhaps using material common to both this story and the above St.Cairnech one and possibly the lost Echtra[43]. Aided can now be found in the existing manuscripts TCD, H 2.16. (Yellow Book of Lecan), cols. 310-320, fourteenth century, TCD, H 2.7., pp. 248-254, fifteenth century, and RIA, 23 O 21, p. 25, nineteenth century. However, the story is also mentioned in the ninth to eleventh centuries *Baile in Scail*,

---

[42] Donnchadha, Lil Nic. Aided Muircertach Meic Erca –, Dublin Institute for advanced studies 1980 and Guyonvarc'h, J. Le Mort De Muirchertach, Fils De Erc, Annales. Économies, Sociétés, Civilisations, Année 1983, Volume 38, Numéro 5 pp. 985 - 1015

[43] Associations with the lost Echtra suggested by Duignan, Leonie, in The Echtrae as an Early Irish Literary Genre 2010, School of Celtic Studies. "*It may be that Aided Muirchertaig Meic Erca is either partially or wholly related to a no longer extant tale entitled Echtra Muirquertoig maic hErco, given the appearance of the otherworld woman Sín to the King Muirchertach of Tara, their subsequent mating and outing to Tech Cletig*"

showing its older provenance. The story presented here is generally dated to the twelfth century in this version in the *Yellow Book of Lecan* although certainly the story pre-dates the advent of the idea of purgatory in the twelfth century as hell is here described as being cold[44].

The original may be of the late tenth century following the death of Muircertach O'Neill in 943 who is described in the annals of Ulster as the *"Hector of the western world"*. In this story, Mac Erca is described in a similar way – *"the high king of the western world"*. The triple death of Mac Erca at Cleitech is also mentioned in a poem called *Fianna Batar I nEmain* by Cinaed Ua hArtacain who died in 975.[45] The usage of old Irish words such as *Boind* for the river Boyne, which had become rare by the year 1000[46] also show the ancient provenance of the story. However, the *Danaraib*, usually said to be *Danes*[47] are mentioned in the story dating this part to the latter part of the tenth century when the first attestation of the word Danair appears in the annals of Ulster between 986 and 990[48]. This does not mean of course that it had not been used earlier. Whoever they were in reality,

---

[44] 'Fearful fearful is the coldness of hell', Ibid Guyonvarc'h, pg.991, who also cites Le Goff, Jacques. The Birth of Purgatory, University of Chicago Press, 1986.

[45] Ibid Dhonnchadha pg. 10 who gives other instances of where the actual wounding is included, as it is in this poem.

[46] *"The use of disyllabic Boind (*river Boyne*) is an early feature that had almost entirely disappeared in Ireland by circa 1000"*. Hudson Benjamin T. Prophecy of Berchan – Irish and Scottish High Kings In the Early Middle Ages, , Praeger Publishers, 1996 Pg. 13.

[47] Dumville casts some doubt on this. Dumville, David N. Celtic Essays, 2001-2007, University of Aberdeen, 2007, pgs.106-107.

[48] Ibid Dumville, pp.106-107.

possibly Scandinavians operating out of Orkney[49], after this they are no longer mentioned. It is possible that as Mac Erca was said in the story of St. Cairnech to have also ruled in Caithness and Orkney that by the mid tenth century with the Danes operating out of, or settled in the area, they were inserted into the story of Mac Erca's triumphs. Indeed, just like the brief mention of them in the annals, in this story he rules them for only two years.

A more defined period for the composition of the tale may come from the fact that the story gives equal footing to both the Cenél Conaill and Cenél Eoghan[50] families of the O'Neill's. This is surprising as Cenél Conaill power had waned to a significant degree by the ninth century in favour of Cenél Eoghan as pointed out by Brian Lacey in his 2006 dissection of the Cenél Conaill kingdoms of the north. There was only a short period where their influence resumed when they appear as the Ua Mael Doraid and the Ua Canannain families in the mid tenth century[51]. It was after the death of Muircertach O'Neill in 943 and Donnchad Donn in 944 - whom his daughter had married - that Ruaidrí ua Canannáin assumed power and may have been High King of Ireland. He died in 950. It is most likely therefore, that Aided was started during this six-year period of Cenél Conaill resurgence. After this, the Cenél Eoghan once more assumed the High Kingship

---

[49] See Downham, Clare Viking Kings Of Britain and Ireland - the dynasty of Ívarr to A.D. 1014, , Dunedin Academic Press 2007, who cites Barbara Crawford.

[50] See Aided MME , para.12

[51] Lacey, Brian. Cenel Conail and the Donegal Kingdoms, Four Courts Press 2006, pg.319.

under Domnall ua Néill and Cenél Conaill power had come to a final end. The story was then embellished and added to in the eleventh and subsequent centuries.

Lil Nic Dhonnchadha[52], in his presentation of the original story considered that the tale was more folkloric in its earlier form and more religious in its later, playing down the three fold death aspect in the later, where the wounding by spear was removed. It is a supernatural tale involving the fairy woman Sin (pronounced Sheen) and her efforts to seduce and kill Mac Erca. The Celtic form of his three fold death is not unique though, very similar deaths being attributed to at least three other Irish kings – Cormac Mac Art, Diarmait Mac Cerbaill and Aed Dub. Its roots have very ancient origins in Indo European tradition. Arthur of course nearly suffers the same fate, being wounded and taken to water (only his sword symbolically drowns) but misses the last fiery exit; instead much like Mac Erca's tale, the pagan 'three fold death' aspect is broken by later Christianisation of his story. Layamon, writing his versified Brut in the early thirteenth century concerning the history of Britain, appears to know of this tale as he incorporates some of its symbolism into his work in the 'fortunes wheel' dream of Arthur where he symbolically makes Arthur survive the triple death![53]

The updated English translation used for this story of Mac Erca's death is based on that by Whitley Stokes, *Aided*

[52] Ibid Donnchadha, see his introduction, pgs. (i) – x.

[53] Layamons Brut, Loomis, Willard. <u>Medieval English Verse and Prose</u>, New York 1948.

Muirchertaig Meic Erca, Revue Celtique 23 (1902) pp. 395–437. This translation however, leaves out most of the verses, which add much more information than the narrative alone gives. I have therefore endeavoured to translate the verses using the French translation by Guyonvarc'h as a guide but with the help of Dhonnchadha's vocabulary list, eDill (Electronic dictionary of the Irish Language) and with the help of the scholars of the Old Irish Language discussion group. I have also left the paragraph numbers intact to make referral to the original Irish source easier. Therefore, presented here for the first time is the full English translation of this story.

Ancestry

Mac Erca's ancestry appears confused and contrived, which is similar to Arthurs but even more complicated. In Arthur's legend, his father Uther changed his appearance by magic to appear as though he were Gorlois, the husband of Igraine. Uther lay with Igraine and Arthur was the result of that union. In effect, Uther has stolen the wife of Gorlois and in the legends he does indeed kill Gorlois and finally marry Igraine. In the Irish legends, Mac Erca's father is said to have done a very similar thing but did not need to change shape to do it! He instead eloped with princess Erc who was betrothed to the King of Britain.

Mac Erca is said to have been either the son of a mother called Erc, who was the daughter of Loarn, a king of Alba (Argyll, Scotland), or the name Erc is said to have been applied to him because he was blessed by Bishop Erc of Slane (a disciple of St.Patrick) , a name much later Anglicised as *Erth*[54] in Cornwall. *Erth* in Welsh can mean *bear*[55] the same meaning as *Arth*. In the Irish Annals in the Cotton MS. Titus A. XXV Mac Erca's name is spelt *Erta* on the notice of his death but this is most likely just scribal error. The idea that he was a son of a mother called Erc is an invention of the tenth to eleventh century when the name Mac

---

[54] Orme, Nicholas The Saints of Cornwall, Oxford University Press, 2000.

[55] Erthgi –'Bear Hound' from the poem 'The Gododdin'. Higham N. J. King Arthur: Myth-making and History 2002. Also Koch, the name Erthyr –'Bear King', The Celtic Culture Enclodpedia, p. 121.

Erca was reinterpreted as a metronymic[56]. Mac Erca was a common enough name in ancient Ireland, there being Mac Erca's of Munster in county Kerry, others in Connaught, called the 'mightiest and firmest'[57] and even others in Anglesey, Wales[58].

His father is said to be Muiredach (obit circa 490), a grandson of the famous Niall of the Nine Hostages (obit circa 450). Muiredach part Irish and even part Saxon[59] is said to have eloped with the Irish princess Erc, daughter of Loarn, King of Argyll. Princess Erc was the prospective wife of Sarran[60], a legendary King of Britain and Ireland and so Sarran had married Babona the other daughter of Loarn. Erc's marriage to Muiredach produced Muircertach, Feradach, Tigernach and Maian. After Muiredach's death, Erc married again, this time to Fergus son of Connal Gulban and produced Sedna, Fedhlim, Brendan and another Loarn. Fedhlim was the father of St Columba the famous founder of the monastery of Iona. This convoluted genealogy created a confusion of brothers, half brothers, uncles and sisters of Muircertach. One of the objectives appears to have been to enable him to be half related to more than one branch of the

---

[56] See Charles Edwards, T.M. The Chronicle of Ireland Vol.1, Liverpool University Press 2006, pg.83 and Smith, B. Ed. Britain and Ireland, 900–1300 Insular Responses to Medieval European Change University of Bristol 1999.

[57] Ibid Byrne Pg. 232. "the mightiest and firmest of the Connachta, but they do not rule like over-kings"

[58] Bodedern parish church. Anglesey. See The Celtic Inscribed Stones Project. http://www.ucl.ac.uk/archaeology/cisp/database/

[59] His father Eoghan is said to have married a Saxon princess.

[60] The Pictish form of this would be 'Tarran' and hence there is a suspicion here that Vortigern – the 'superbus tyrannus' is implied.

O'Neills - the Cenél Conaill and the Cenél Eoghan; the Cenél Conaill actually having been the more powerful in the sixth century.[61]

Mac Erca's children, from his first wife include one Baedan whose descendents become rulers of Saxon Northumbria in the seventh century (Aldfrid). On a more mythical level, from his second wife (the daughter of Clovis!!), he is made to be the father of Constantine, the same as mentioned by the British historian Gildas in the sixth century and hence the progenitor of the Kings of the Britons. It appears the Irish wanted to cover all bases by trying to make Mac Erca's descendents the legitimate rulers of Ireland, Scotland, Britain and France!! Much like Geoffrey of Monmouth tried to do with King Arthur.

---

[61] See full discussion by Lacey, Brian. Cenel Conail and the Donegal Kingdoms 500-800. Four Courts Press, 2006, pp.187 – 205.

The Name

The word *Erc(a)* can mean 'heaven or sky'[62] and so Mac Erca - 'son of the sky/heaven'[63] and hence literally a 'star'. *Erca* is said to be related to the Sanskrit *'Arka'* – ray, sun, star[64] and possibly also to Sanskrit *arća*, Greek *Arktos*, Latin *Urcsus* > *Ursus* – 'bear' and hence some association with the star Arcturus in the constellation Boötes could be suggested. Arcturus is a red star and indeed 'Erc' can also mean 'red'[65] suggesting *Mac Erca* could have been the Goidelic form of this stars name.

John MacNeill in his work *The History and Grammar of Ogham Inscriptions* says of Erca that the name is *"frequent as a female name in legendary material"*.[66] In the *Proceedings of the Royal Irish Academy* 1931 (p.38) there is a suggestion that the name Erca is associated with a Goddess:

"Erca was the name, perhaps rather the byname of a God or Goddess. A byname is more likely, since no Erc has been found

---

[62] Cormacs glossary, ninth century, Erc i. nem. (Erc meaning heaven/sky). Also see eDil, Electronic Dictionary of the Irish Language - http://www.dil.ie/index.asp, for other examples such as O'Davoren's Glossary and the On the metrical glossaries of the mediæval Irish, Stokes, Whitley, MRIA (1830-1909).

[63] First suggested by MacNeill, John. History and Grammar of Ogham Inscriptions, Proceedings of the Royal Irish Academy, House of Dubros,1909.

[64] See Pictet (circa 1859) (Kuhn's Zeitschrift, iv. 355) who has compared this word to Skr. *Arka* 'ray' 'sun', also Allen, Richard H. Star Names: Their Lore and Meaning, Dover Publications, 2000 and Müller, Friedrich Max. Lectures on The Science Of Languages, 1862 p.378.

[65] eDil – "speckled, also dark red: earc .i. breac no ní breac, O'Cl. .i. dearg ib. alath, odhar, usgdha, erc, irfind (the vowels in dath-ogam)."

[66] Ibid MacNeill, History and Grammar of Ogham Inscriptions, pp.357-8.

prominent in the mythological tradition; and the very frequent personal name Mac Erce, MAQI ERCIAS, "son (by dedication?) of Erca," points to a protecting goddess. "

The meaning therefore could in fact be *son of the goddess Ursus,* or *son of the bear.* In Greek legend, it was Arcas, son of Ursus who was sent to the sky by Zeus to form the constellation of *Boötes* to prevent Arcas from killing his mother.[67] The brightest star in Boötes is Arcturus and eventually, by the seventh century, Arcas, Ursus and Arcturus were wrapped up under the one banner of Arcturus.

The hypothetical fifth century masculine genitive of Erca would be **Ercas,* the feminine being *Ercias*[68]. Boötes also sits closest to the constellation of Draco – the Dragon, a creature much associated with Arthur's family the *Pendragons.* Graham Anderson in his 2003 work, *Arthur in Antiquity,* relates the full analysis of Arcas and Arcturus and their links with Arthurian legend.[69] This association of Mac Erca with a star is further reinforced in one of the final verses in *Aided* where an angel is reciting words concerning Mac Erca[70] :

You have gone to the sky Mac Erca
Above us now for our fervent prayer

---

[67] Ibid Anderson.

[68] See below for more details on Ercias from Ogham inscriptions.

[69] For a full discussion on Arthurs links with Arcturus see Anderson, Graham. Arthur in Antiquity, Routledge, 2003.

[70] Aided para 51 – verse.

You have gone, forever on high.

With your bright body that belongs in hell.

These words do suggest that Mac Erca was associated with a star much like the Latin panegyrics of famous Romans that also made such associations[71]. In this poem, as well as being placed in the sky, his body is described in much the same way as a star is, '*bright*' and just like the star Arcturus which never sets, he is said to be '*forever on high*'. *Arcturus* was a name frequently used in place of the form *Arthur* by medieval writers such as Geoffrey of Monmouth who did so in *The Prophecies of Merlin*. Arcturus is also one of the few names that could naturally evolve into the name *Arthur* quite regularly: Arcturus – Arthurus - Arthur.

The word *Erc* however, has many meanings in Goidelic each of which we will examine in a later work and suggest how they may have influenced Arthurian legends. In Welsh though *Erc /Erch(an)*[72] could mean 'terrible' or 'horrible'. In the *Sawley Gloss*[73], a 13th century gloss in the HB, Arthur's name was glossed with the words:

---

[71] See Claudians Panagyrics in <u>The Barbarian Invasions of the Roman Empire, Vol.1, The Visigothic Invasions</u>. Thomas Hodgkin, The Clarendon Press 1880. Reprinted by The Folio Society, London, 2000.

[72] See Ercagni in <u>Inscribed Stones Project</u> where "White/1971-72, 46--51, cites personal communications from K. Jackson and M. Richards, arguing that *Ercagni* is from Latin **Ercagnus* or British **Ercagnos* giving *Erchan* in Welsh". Of course, it could just be the diminutive of Erce as in the Goidelic Ercéne. The point though is that there would have been some confusion as there is now.

[73] Gidlow, Christopher, <u>The Reign Of Arthur From History to Legend</u>, Sutton Publishing Ltd., 2004. See also Dumville's Pseudo Histories for fuller discussion.

"Mabuter, that is horrible son, since from his boyhood he was cruel. Arthur translated into Latin means "horrible bear" or "iron hammer", with which the jaws of lions were broken"

The word *Uther* had a similar meaning of *horrible* or *terrible*. *MabUter* therefore could have been a direct transliteration from the Goidelic *Mac Erca*. Mac Erca's wife is named in the sources as Duinsech or Duibsech (brown haired girl/daughter) which in Welsh would be *Gwinau-verch*. The similarity of this to the name *Guinevere* requires no further elucidation at this time.

Muircertach itself as a name is split into '*Muir*' – 'the sea', or 'from overseas' and *Certach/Certhach*. *Cert* is an Irish word meaning 'correct' or 'right' but as a compound with *muir* doesn't appear to make sense and *cert* always appears as a prefix, not a suffix[74]. *Certach* could be the Irish version of the late Welsh name *Ceredig / Keretic* from the earlier Careticus and the same as St. Patricks Latin version Coroticus and the eighth-century possibility *Coirthech*[75]. The meaning of the root of Careticus, is *loving, dear* which is essentially the same root as in the name Caratacus and the Irish equivalent names Carthach and Carthir[76] and their much later variations McCarthy and MacArthur. Muircertach is later spelt *Muircerthach*[77] showing the possibility

[74] eDil. Electronic Dictionary of the Irish Language.

[75] Dumville suggests some doubt to this being a genuine Irish name form. Saint Patrick AD 493-1993.

[76] Kenneth H. Jackson, "Queen Boudicca?", *Britannia* 10 p. 255, 1979, se also Dumville et al, *Saint Patrick 493-1993*.

[77] '*Muircherthach* Ua Briain' from the Annals of The Four Masters.

of this relationship. The meaning then, would be something like *Sea lover*[78]. However, there are other possibilities which will be discussed later concerning the name *Muircertach* which appears very similar to the word *Murchorthach* glossed in MS as meaning '*a foreigner from overseas'*, particularly a Briton[79]. In English the name *Muircertach* eventually evolved into the name *Moriarty*.

Proving the historicity of *Muircertach* would be difficult based only on the existing evidence from old Irish manuscripts and king lists. Although one *Mac Ercéne* is listed as an early sixth century king in the late seventh century Irish king list in the *Baile Chuinn Chétchathaig* (The Frenzy of Conn of the hundred battles) it is not clear that *Muircertach Mac Muiredaig* is meant even though the later tales make them one[80]. Certainly the exploits of '*Mac Erca'* were known to Cenn Faelad, a seventh century poet and descendent[81] of Mac Erca if the attributions to him are sound. The name '*Muircertach'* appears to be a later addition to the name and person of '*Mac Erca'* instigated by the O'Neill clan in

---

[78] Which appears to be supported by MacLysaght, The Surnames of Ireland, who suggests '*navigator'*; and O' Corrain & Maguire Irish Names, 2nd edition (Dublin, Ireland: Lilliput Press, 1990), who suggest '*skilled in seacraft, mariner'*; and Woulfe, Irish Names and Surnames, who suggests '*sea-director, mariner'*.

[79] Murchorthach, 'coming from overseas' eDill, gloss on the word 'cu-glas' from the Law Tracts on Díre, early eighth century, also spelt muirchuirthe – literally vomit of the sea - a man stranded from the sea. See Satirical Narrative in Early Irish Literature, Ailís Ní Mhaoldomhnaigh, School Of Celtic Studies 2007. Older form of cu glas would be Cuneglase. See also The Social Background to Irish Perigrinatio, T.M. Charles-Edwards pgs. 46-47

[80] T. M. Charles-Edwards, Early Christian Ireland (Cambridge University Press, 2000) p.490 calls him "..half legendary". His O'Neill pedigree is probably an invention of the C8th - C9th. See High Kings and Pipe Dreams, Laurance J. Maney, Proceedings Of The Harvard Celtic Colloqium 24, 2004.

[81] Cen Faelad, son of Ailill, son of Baitan, son of Mac Erca., Ibid Lacey pg.300.

the eighth to ninth centuries. It is in the ninth century that we find the next mention of the name Muircertach in the Irish Annals as kings in Ireland[82]. This suggests that the story of Muircertach's heroic exploits were sufficiently known by the ninth century so that kings would name their sons after him.

'*Muircertach Mac Erca*' is first mentioned in full in the king list in the ninth to eleventh centuries *Baile in Scáil* (the Book of the Phantoms Frenzy) amongst the O'Neill high kings of the sixth century in the place originally occupied by Mac Ercéne. The *Baile In Scail* survives in fifteenth and sixteenth century manuscripts; the Oxford Bodleian Library, Rawlinson B. 512 and British Library, Harley 5280. The king list, revised in the ninth century in favour of the O'Neills, was based on that in *Baile Chuinn Chétchathaig* and ends with Congal Cennmagair who died according to the Annals in 710 but the list was continued and added to at later times up to the eleventh century[83]. At this time it was more fully revised in favour of the O'Neill's by Abbot Dub-Da-Leithe of Armagh[84]. In this Muircertach is said to be the son of the daughter of Loarn[85] and the story of his death at Cleitech[86] is also mentioned.

---

[82] Annals of Ulster, year 805. 'Muirchertach son of Donngal, king of Bréifne, died'. Year 926 'Muirchertach son of Niall' inflicted a rout on the foreigners...'

[83] Kevin Murray –'Baile in Scail And Baile Bricin', Eiglise, vol. XXXIII, 2002. National University of Ireland. Also see CMCS, 55 Summer 2008 pgs 75-78 in a review of 'Baile in Scail 'The Phantoms Frenzy'',Kevin Murray, 2004, Irish Texts society by Liam Breatnach, Dublin Institute of Advanced Studies.

[84] Prophecy Of Berchan, Benjamin T Hudson, Praeger Publishers, 1996, Pg 97.

[85] 'Dáil de for Muircertach mac Ercoi, id est ingen Loairn.

[86] Íer sin línfus co h-Érind airbiu. Benuid dubuirt hi mairt in cairb coscrach col-Laigniu.

The earliest forms of the name '*Mac Erca*' are from Ogham inscriptions on standing stones in Wales and Ireland dated to the fifth and sixth centuries. The name on these take the forms 'maqi Ercagni' and 'maqi Ercias' which is reflected in the earliest manuscript evidence for Mac Erca, the *Baile Chuinn*, from the 670's which uses the diminutive *Mac Ercéne*. There is also Ogham evidence for *Erca* but the dating of this can be as late as the eighth century so is ignored. The form *Ercéne* then is quite archaic in the *Baile Chuinn* MS and is a fairly rare diminutive in old Irish showing its ancient provenance and the probability of it being an authentic entry. The Ogham feminine *a*-stem *Maqqi Ercias* is the form most likely to evolve into Mac Erce > Mac Erca. [87] The suffix '*ias*' is a feminine genitive termination[88]. A masculine form if it existed, corresponding to *Ercias*, would be **Ercas* although *Erc* itself as a male name exists on an early standing stone showing both the male and female aspects of the similar names - ERC MAQI MAQI-ERCIA[S MU] DOVI[N]IA[89], which translates as *Erc son of Mac-Erce of the tribe of Duibne*. The Corco Duibne are a county Kerry tribe and indeed this is where the stone was found.

Mór atbai. Beab*aid* M*u*rcer*tach* écc atbai mairt Cletigh.

[87] See The Celtic Inscriptions of Britain: Phonology and Chronology, c. 400-1200 Patrick Sims-Williams, Wiley-Blackwell, 2002 for fuller discussion on the various forms of Erc.

[88] History and Grammar of Ogham Inscriptions. By John MacNeil, Proceedings of the Royal Irish Academy, 1909, pp 357-8."

[89] CISP Database - http://www.ucl.ac.uk/archaeology/cisp/database/

In the late seventh century Adamnan mentions the name as Mac *Erce* in the *Vita (Life) of St Columba*. Around the same time the authors of St Patrick's Vitae used the same form *Erce*. In the Irish annals, the earliest form indicated appears to be *Erce* with *Erca* and *Ercae* appearing to be later orthographic and phonological developments of the mid eighth century onwards[90]. This all suggests that the earliest Annal witness to the name is from a late seventh to early eighth century exemplar or this was the time when some of the Annal entries were written.

---

[90] Language of The Annals OF Ulster, Tomas O Maille, Manchester University Press, 1910, pgs 55-56. The development appears to be Ercias > Erce > Ercae > Erca. "*The final -e of a-stems is not Indo-Germanic, but is an innovation in Irish. It comes from - ias or es. There are certain analogies for both: Ogham g.Ercias (Macalister, iii. p. 152), g. of Erc ; cf. g. Erce 560.* ibid O Maille.

Mac Erca and Muircertach Mac Muiredaig

It is clear that the O'Neill's associated the 'shadowy figure' of *Muircertach Mac Muiredaig* of their genealogies with *Mac Ercéne*[91] the historical king who is also mentioned by Adamnan as *Mac Erce* in the late seventh century Life of St. Columba. In that Life is mentioned a battle in which Domnall and Forcus, two sons of (Muircertach) Mac Erce took part and were victors[92]. In this battle, called Cul Dreimne, noted in the Annals of Ulster for the year 560/61, the original entry just contained the name form *Mac Ercae* but at a later point, the name *Muircertach* was added. This shows that the entry was most likely mined from Adamnan and was then added to later, hence the original entry is late eighth century[93] and the addition most likely ninth or later. King lists, Annals and legends subsequent to the ninth century, now fully influenced by the O'Neill's, mention him as '*Muircertach Mac Erca*' from then on[94].

---

[91] Irish Kings and High Kings. Francis J Byrne, Four Courts Press 2001, pg. 102. Ercéne is a diminutive form of Erca. Byrne calls Muircertach Mac Muiredaig a shadowy figure.

[92] The Annals of Ulster, AT and others. See Cenel Conail and the Donegal Kingdoms, Brian Lacey, Four Courts Press 2006.

[93] Note the form '*Ercae*' at 762 and 773 in the Annals of Ulster. Ibid O'Maille, Pg.79. However an earlier spelling of 'Erce' exists in the AI relating to this battle but it contains a mix of Latin and old Irish suggesting a similar or later date as it mentions Muircertach in relation to Mac Erca. *Mors da h-ua Muirchertaich, .i. Boetan macc Meicc Erce & Eochaid mc. Domnaill meicc Meicc Erce*

[94] For most of the Annal material see Chronicles and Annals of Medieval Ireland & Wales, Kathryn Grabowski and David Dumville, The Boydell Press, 1984.

How or why Muircertach Mac Muiredaig became associated with Mac Ercéne is difficult to explain. If, as surmised by Byrne (1973), Dáibhí Ó Cróinín (2003)[95] and more fully by Maney (2004) and Lacey (2006)[96], it was an eighth to ninth century O'Neill ploy to link him with their Cenél[97] Eoghan dynasty then we have the equally puzzling question remaining as to who exactly was Mac Erca? Adamnan writing in the late seventh century mentions Mac Erca twice:

"These kings were known as Ainmore, son of Setna, and the two sons of Mac Erce, Domnall and Forcus"

"A Prophecy of the blessed man regarding two other Kings, who were called the two descendants (nepotes) of Muiredach, Baitan, son of Mac Erce, and Eochoid, son of Domnall".

In these, we can see that there is confirmation that Baitan, Domnall and Forcus are sons of Mac Erca and Echoid is his grandson. Maney suggests the second statement presumably[98] links Mac Erca with the Cenél Feradaig of the Cenél Eoghan ancestor Muiredach Mac Eoghan. This means that in Adamnan's time, those whom he knew as *'fili Mac Erce'* (sons of Mac Erce) claimed descent from Muiredach Mac Eoghan Mac Niall. Cenél

[95] Ireland ,400-800 - A New History of Ireland Vol.1 2008.

[96] Ibid Byrne pg. 102 . See also High Kings and Pipe Dreams, Laurance J. Maney, Proceedings Of The Harvard Celtic Colloqium 24, 2004, pgs. 256-260., Also ibid Lacey.

[97] *'Cenél'* means , kindred, tribe, race. eDill.

[98] As this is not explicitly stated there is no guarantee that this Muiredach was the son of Eoghan. See Lacey ibid for fuller discussion.

Mac Ercae then, Maney suggests, as a separate entity to Cenél Feradaig/Eoghan, did not exist at this time. In support of this argument Maney shows that Cenél Mac Ercae were absent from the list of guarantors[99] of Adamnan's Law in the late seventh century but the Cenél Feredaig were not.

From the early eighth century though, Cenél Feradaig power had effectively ended[100] and to such an extent that the Cenél Eoghan clan sought to separate themselves from them. By the mid to late eighth century, with the defeat of Cenél Conaill in 789 at the battle of Cloitech[101], they created their O'Neill identity by merging an ancestor of theirs called Muircertach Mac Muiredaig with Mac Ercene of the *Bail Chuinn* king list and hence created a more powerful Cenél Mac Ercae ancestor devoid of the Mac Muiredaig patronymic.[102] This is then reflected in the ninth century *Baile in Scáil* king list where he is finally called *Muircertach Mac Erca*. Mac Erca's sons Domnall and Fergus were therefore now raised in the *Baile in Scáil* king list and made into 'High Kings of Tara' when they did not exist in the earlier Baile Chuinn High King list, but were more likely just kings of Ailech.

---

[99] The guarantors were, Cenél Conaill, Cenél Feradaig of Cenél nEoghan, Cenél Cairpre, Eoganacht Aine, Eoganacht Locha Lein, Osraige, Deissi, Ui Fidgeinte, Deissi in Tuaiscairt, Eogonacht Raithlind and Eogonacht Glendamnach.

[100] Ibid Lacey Pg.272 and Maney.

[101] Ibid Lacey p110. The Cenél Conaill were then excluded from the over kingship of the 'northern O'Neill' and the Cenél Eoghan territory known as In Fochla (the north) increasingly became known as the 'kingdom of Ailech'.

[102] Ibid Maney, pgs. 256-260

In essence then, we have two shadowy figures that have been merged; an early sixth century king called Mac Ercéne about whom practically nothing is known apart from late seventh century reports that his father's name was Muiredach, he defeated Lugaide in battle and according to the annals fought twelve or more. He became king, his sons were kings and later legends made him a great warrior; and Muircertach Mac Muiredaig about whom again, nothing is known apart from his later merged legends of the eighth to ninth centuries. The latter of these appears to have been a sort of drunken gentle chap, the former a martial hero adopted into the genealogies of the O'Neill's.

The Annals of Innisfallon and Ulster
Mac Erca's Battles

The oldest Irish Annal MS in existence, the eleventh century *Annals of Innisfallen* (AI) from Munster, southern Ireland, appears to retain the earliest notices of Mac Erca's battles. These entries all appear in Latin, where he is only called *Mac Erce* (except for one instance, see below) showing their early provenance and lack of contamination from O'Neill propaganda in the northern *Annals of Ulster* (AU) which had split from the original Iona chronicle in the mid eighth century[103]. They give us some idea of which other battles may have been later attributions to Mac Erca in divergent annals. Of these battles, the ones most likely to be original to Mac Erce were Gránaird in 486, Inní Móir circa 500, Segaisse circa 502, Cinn Eich and Atha Sighe circa 530 and Eblinne circa 532. Adding sub battles to two of these campaigns mentioned in other annals we could then add the battles of Delg, Mucremhe and Tuaim Drubha in 500 and Muighi Ailbe, Aidne, and Almuine in 532 making a total of twelve, the same number as Arthur is attributed in his wars against the Saxons.

The entries in the *Annals of Ulster* retaining the older spelling of *Erce* also agree with these battles listed in the AI. In one place

---

[103] Koch, <u>Celtic Culture, A Historical Encyclopedia Vol.</u>1 pg.71.

in AI, concerning the date 530, one battle, Atha Sighe was attributed to Muircertach and another, Cenn Eich to Mac Erce as though they were separate characters but this may just reflect an error in the AI. The entry concerning these two battles in the AU merges the two names as victors of both or this is how they were originally. The battles then, which appear to be later attributions to Mac Erca, are Ocha (484), Cell Osnada (489), and Detnae (520).

It has been suggested by many commentators that one battle of Mac Erca's, *Grainaird* in 486, could have been a later attribution to him in place of Coirpre Mac Neill who was given the first credit in the AU[104]. However, in the AI, Mac Erce is given first credit and then Coirpre is mentioned[105], which would be strange if the AU was the original. The AU entry also uses the formula *fili Erce* instead of *Mac Erce* and also uses the spelling *Granaerad,* (with *ae* for *ai*) a ninth century onwards form[106]. This could mean then, that the attribution to Coirpre is actually a later addition than that of Mac Erca's.

It has been suggested by Lacey[107] and others that *Mac Erca son of Ailil Molt* may instead have fought the early battles in 500 and 502. This seems unlikely, as this *Mac Erca* did not die until

---

[104] For instance see Byrne, Francis J. Irish Kings and High Kings. Four Courts Press, 2000.

[105] Bellum Gránaird Meicc Erce uictor, in quo cecidit Finnchad rí Laigen, & Corpre uictor ut alii dicunt. "The battle of Gránaird, Mac Erce victor, in which Finnchad, king of the Laigin, fell; and Cairpre [was] victor, as others say"

[106] Ibid MacNeil –The language of the Annals of Ulster.

[107] Ibid pp.168-170

548 according to the AU so he may have been too young in 500 to be a battle leader and he is always quantified as *the son of Ailil Molt* in the Annals.

Surprisingly this analysis of his battles shows Muircertach Mac Erca to have been absent from any in Ireland for nearly thirty years between 502 and 530. In later verse this is the precise time he was said to have been in Britain in command of the armies of the Britons and Saxons.[108]

There is no note of Mac Erca's death in the AI, the earliest note appearing in the AU in Latin for the year 534 using the form *Muirchertaig Filii Erce*. Using the word *fili* however instead of Mac/Meic, which would be more regular, suggests it is a late addition especially as it gives his merged name and ancestry and expands on the story of his death at Cleitech[109]. For the notices of his death, the AU appears to show an early spelling of *Erce* in the first of the two notices of his death[110], one in 534.1 and one in 536.5. This latter date appears to coincide with the time of Samhain when Mac Erca is supposed to have died in later myth suggesting this is a post tenth century entry. The earlier entry of 534 shows the early spelling but may not be significant as it mentions his merged name and ancestry. The notices on the start of his reign all appear to be late retrospective additions with the

---

[108] Aided Muircertach Mac Erca – para. 44, verse.

[109] Demersio Muirchertaig filii Erce, .i. Muirchertaigh mc. Muireadhaidh mc. Eoghain mc. Neill Naoighiallaigh, in dolio pleno uino in arxe Cletig supra Boinn

[110] *Demersio Muirchertaig filii Erce, .i. Muirchertaigh mc. Muireadhaidh mc. Eoghain mc. Neill Naoighiallaigh, in dolio pleno uino in arxe Cletig supra Boinn*

earliest Latin version being in the AU for the year 513[111]. In the AI there is no note of the start of his reign or of his death.

Before going into more detail of the manuscript, historical and contemporary evidence which will be dealt with in a larger work I will instead now relate the full *Life and Death of Muircertach Mac Erca* sourced from all the manuscripts that I could find on this person, a story which has never been written in its entirety before[112]. I have kept it to the style of a chronicle in the telling and resisted adding extraneous material as much as is possible except where it is from other Irish manuscripts and concerns events, places or people in the story. The main basis of this story is taken from *`Of The Miracles of Cairnech Here'* (M in references) and all events detailed within should be taken as coming from this source unless referenced.

The second part of the story, concerning *`The Violent Death of Muircertach Mac Erca'* comes from the story of the same name from the Yellow Book of Lecan. All of the battle entries and some of the battle poems are from the Irish and Scottish Annals and most of the dating within the story is taken from D.P. McCarthy's, *Chronological synchronisation of the Irish Annals'*, 2005[113]. Slight adjustments to his dating are required to enable

---

[111] *Muirchertach mc. Earca regnare incipit*

[112] There is a reference in the Annals of Clonmacnoise (C17th) of such a life and death where he is said to be 15 feet tall. In Aided M.M.Erca he is said to have been 30 feet tall. In other words he was seen as a giant in a similar way that King Arthur was. Other more recent authors have also summarised his life such as Lacey 2006 ibid.

[113] https://www.cs.tcd.ie/Dan.McCarthy/chronology/synchronisms/annals-chron.htm Chronological Synchronisation of the Irish Annals,D.P. Mc Carthy, Department of Computer Science, Trinity College, Dublin 2.21 March 2005.

the correct chronological order of the story and as all dates during this period were retrospectively added, a reconciliation of dating is full of pitfalls.

These tales are set in Northern Ireland, Scotland and Northern Britain. In Ireland the main settings are Donegal, Ulster, Meath, Leinster and Munster. The main families concerned are the O'Neills of Ireland both Southern and northern, descendents of Niall of the Nine Hostages and his sons Eoghan and Conall, and the respective descendents of these sons. In Scotland, the setting is Argyll, Strathclyde and lowland Scotland as far as Whitehorn and Cumbria. Of the Britons, those involved are of the family of Sarran and Lew – Lugaide (Louie) in Goidelic and their descendents and the descendents of Mac Erca in Northumbria and Britain.

The Life of Muircertach Mac Erca

Sarran[114], son of Colchu[115], King of Britain, who also held power over the Picts and Saxons was betrothed to Erc daughter of Loarn[116] Mor Mac Erca, king of Alba[117] who had been blessed by St. Patrick along with his brothers Fergus and Aengus.[118] Before the betrothal could be cemented however, Muiredach[119] son of Eoghan[120], son of Niall fell in love with Erc and the two eloped

---

[114] Sarran/Saran father of St Cairnech. In Welsh known as Carun or Corun (Tonsured) , father of St.Carannog in Harleian MS.4181, Hafod Ms.16, Iolo MSS and in Peniarth MS.12'. In other MS and Vita, Corun is Caronnog's brother. In this tale both these saints are equated as will become evident. St Carranog or Carantoc is of course associated in his Vita with King Arthur. Saran, in Tripartite life of Patrick, has 12 sons, he rejected Patrick but his brother Connia received Patrick, has another brother Nadslaugh. Saran bore off captives from Dal Riada and Bishop Olcan promised Saran a place in heaven if he would release them. This angered Patrick who ordered his charioteer to ride over Olcan but he refused.

[115] See The Lives of The British Saints: The Saints of Wales, Cornwall and Irish Saints Vol 2, By S. Baring-Gould, John Fisher, Honourable Society of Cymmrodorion, Kessinger Publishing, 2005. Coelchu (old Irish?) = Colga(n.) Caelbad in St.Patricks Tripartite Life.

[116] Loarn, historical king of Alba. Adomnan, Book of Leinster, Rawl B.502, Senchus Fer nAlban

[117] Alban in M, Alba at first meaning all of Britain, then later Scotland - David Dumville -"Ireland and Britain in Tain Bo Fraich", 1996, but in this tale meaning mainly Scotland/Strathclyde and Argyll.

[118] Lebor Bretnach. Three sons of Erc who obtained the blessing of Patrick –Loarn, Fergus, Aongus.

[119] Mentioned by Adomnan so most likely historical :"A Prophecy of the blessed man regarding two other kings, who were called the two grandsons of Muiredach; Baitan son of Mac Erce, and Eochoid, son of Domnall."

[120] Eoghan's wife Marb (which is a strange name meaning 'Dead' probably in a spiritual sense, hence a pagan) is said to be the daughter of a Saxon King. Banshenchus – 'Lore of Women' making Muiredach half Saxon. Niall, Eoghans father is also said to be a son of a Saxon – Cairen but this is unlikely and more possibly Cairen was a Romano Briton as suggested by T. F. O'Rahilly, Early Irish History and Mythology, 1946, Chapter 12. Metrical Dinshenchus call Cairen a Pict suggesting she was more Brittonic as the Britons north of Hadrian's Wall were all considered Picts or Cruithne.

together to Ireland where they had four sons, Muircertach, Feradhach, Tigernach and Moan. King Sarran instead took Babona the other daughter of Loarn and had many sons namely Lugaide[121], St. Cairnech[122], Bishop Dallain, and Caemlach. Sarran was king of Britain for ten years[123], after which he retired to the church and died in triumph in the House of Martin at Whitehorn.[124] His son, St.Cairnech was then Bishop thereof.

Erc, the daughter of unsubdued Loarn,

The mother of eight great brave sons,

Whose seed has been powerful within,

Between Eoghan and Conall.

Tigernach, who rules with bravery

And Feradach of Kingly power,

Muircertach and Moan, rich in mead,

Were the sons of Erc by Muiredach.

---

[121] Luirig in M. This appears to be composed of 'Louie' - Lugaide in Goidelic and 'rig' – king. In old Welsh personal names Liugui, Legui, Leui, Middle Welsh Llywy. Old Breton Louui, Leugui. See The Celtic Inscriptions of Britain, Phonology and Chronology c400-1200, Patrick Simms-Williams, December 2002, Wiley-Blackwell, pg.193.

[122] The Genealogies of the Irish Saints in Irish Texts iii. P.97, give fathers name as Luithech which appears to reflect an early Goidelic genitive spelling of Lugaide - *Luigdech* . This could be a mistake for Lugaide (Luirig),his brother.

[123] Senchus Fer nAlban, 7th-10th Century. J. M. P. Calise, Pictish Sourcebook : Documents of Medieval Legend and Dark Age History / (Westport, CT: Greenwood Press, 2002).

[124] House of Martin in M = Whitehorn. The Place names of Argyle – H. Cameron Gillies.

The race of Tigernach of rich domains

Are the Siol Tigernach Mac Erce,

Feradach too, a full ripe chief,

From whom are the Cenél Feradaig.

Cenél Moan of the mead

From Moan, son of Muiredach,

Muircertach, the gentle and merry

From him descend the kings of Ailech.

Those are the descendants of the four gentle sons,

Whom Erc left in Tir-Eoghain,

Now I shall name for you without fail,

The descendants of Erc's sons in Tir Chonaill.

The Erc, who sons these were,

Was the daughter of Loarn of Alba:

Whom Fergus, the son of Conall

Took to wife, for dowry after Muiredach.[125]

Muiredach, Muircertach's father, had been carried off as a slave to Alba when a boy but had escaped seven years later after killing his captor Eocho Abratchain Mac Ecuid and then eloped with princess Erc to Ireland[126]. When Muiredach had died, the

---

[125] From a poem beginning "Enna the pupil of hardy Cairbre" cited by Tod and Algernon in 1848 –The Irish Version of the Historia Brittonum. Poem probably by Flann Mainistrech, Eleventh century.

widowed Erc now married Fergus, son of Conal Gulban, son of Niall and gave birth to more sons – Fedhlimidh, father of St Columba, Sedna, Brendain and Loarn[127].

Towards the end of her life, Erc in penitence went to Cairnech to confess her sins and her penitence was so great that she knelt at every second ridge from Tory Island all the way to where he resided at Ross Ailigh. As she approached Cairnech, a due of blood was appearing at the tips of every one of her fingers. He saw her suffering and declared, "I hail thee O Erc, thou shalt certainly go to heaven and one of every two worthy kings who shall reign over Erin shall be of thine seed. The best women and the best clerics shall be theirs and success in battle and combat shall be upon them." Shortly after, Erc's spirit passed over into eternal glory. In her Will, she had bequeathed her territory in Drumleen in Tir Connell [128] to Cairnech; also, her gold, horses, cattle, apparel, and she made sure that her sons paid tribute to Cairnech and his Church every year in the same manner. This they did honourably and it was even paid by descendants of Eoghan for twenty years after Cairnech's death.[129]

---

[126] Aided Muircertach Meic Erca –Lil Nic Donnchadha, Dublin Institute for advanced studies 1980. p12 citing a poem by Flann Mainstrech (Died circa 1056). See also Poems by Flann Mainistrech on the Dynasties of Ailech, Mide and Brega : Flann Mainistrech and John MacNeil, Archivium Hibernicum, Vol. 2 (1913)

[127] As above p.12 citing Todd who cites Colgan and Ogygia. Probably though just a confusion of the Ercs.

[128] Land of the people of Conn. Later called Donegal after the Vikings had settled (post 9th century).

[129] The story of Erc's penitence and death from a poem beginning "Enna the pupil of hardy Cairbre" cited by Tod and Algernon in 1848 –The Irish Version of the Historia Brittonum..

Feargus, the son of great Muircertach,

With his noble, illustrious great sons,

Took the Druim[130] subject to this tribute

Hence, they were called Fir Droma.

Meanwhile Muircertach, when a young boy in Ireland was blessed by Bishop Erc of Slane[131], a disciple of St. Patrick and some say that is how he acquired his name of *Mac Erca* meaning a 'son of heaven'[132]. It was said of Bishop Erc that:

Whatever he adjusted was right.

Whoever judges justly and fairly

Will receive the blessing of Bishop Erc. [133]

At the age of seven Mac Erca then spent ten years under the tutelage of Saigen the Druid as his foster father. For two years after this, he spent time with his father Muiredach[134], the great and illustrious King of Ailech who reigned for twenty-four years.[135]

---

[130] Druim Lighean – modern Drumleen.

[131] Death mentioned in 513 in AT, AU and CS. 'The Chronicle of Ireland', T.M. Charles Edwards, 2005, Liverpool University Press. Pg.87

[132] 'A son of the heavens' ie possibly meaning 'a Star' in heaven. See eDILL for meanings of Erc. See also Pictet (circa 1859) (Kuhn's Zeitschrift, iv. 355) who has compared this word to Skr. *Arka* 'ray' 'sun'. Possibly an origin for the association with Arcturus –Arturus –Arthur.

[133] ' George Petrie, 'On the history and antiquities of Tara Hill', Transactions of the Royal Irish Academy 18 (1839), 25–232: 251'. This blessing and poem said to be from the Book of Lecan, fol. 306, p. a. col. 1. Whether this tale is earlier than the invented association with a mother called Erc is hard to say. One attaches Muircertach to Mac Erca, the other Mac Erca to Muircertach. It would seem illogical though to make up a story of Bishop Erc later than the story of him being a son of a mother called Erc?

After the retirement of Sarran, Lugaid[136] became king of Dal Araidhe, Strathclyde and Britain and extended his power over the Saxons but he was a pagan and did not fear God. He started to build a fort within the grounds of the monastery of Cairnech his brother which displeased Cairnech greatly.

Meanwhile, Muircertach Mac Erca as a young Lord of Ailech of the Northern Irish clan of Niall allied himself with his uncle Lugaid of the Dál Aráidhe Clan to expand their territory into the land of their own kin in Connaught. In Meath they allied with Fergus Cerball and Fiachra Lon and defeated and killed Oilill Molt of Connaught in the great battle of Ocha in 484. [137]

The great battle of Ocha was fought,

Through which many fights were contested;

Over Oilill Molt, son of Dathi,

It was gained by the Dál Aráidhe,

By Lugaide, by Fiachra Lonn,

And by the great, puissant Muircertach,

---

[134] Aided Muircertach Mac Erca. Para 44. Fosterage could begin as early as one year to seven years old. Mac Erca would have been around seventeen when he had finished. He then spent two years with his father. His first battle is supposed to be that of Ocha in 484 meaning he would have had to be finished with his fosterage by Saigen and spent two years with his father leaning the ropes. So if he was 19 in 484 he would have been born in around 465 and his age at death would be somewhere around 70-73 in 534-37. In the poem though he states he lived one hundred and ten years, obviously mythical as much of this work is.

[135] Book of Leinster poem by Flann Mainistrech. Meaning Muiredach started his reign in 466 and his father Eoghan who reigned for twenty years takes us back to 446, the time that Niall died.

[136] The 'Loth/Lot' of Geoffrey of Monmouth and 'Lew' of the Welsh Bruts.

[137] Possibly from Ech / Eocha – horse, probably not Ocha – armpit? DIL Irish Lexicon.

By Fergus, son of mild Conall—
By them fell the noble King Ailill;
And by Fergus of the blemish—
By them fell the noble Ailill Molt.[138]

Then with his other uncle Coirpre in 485 fought in the battle of Grainne [139] where Finnchad fell.

And the battle of Grainne over Finnchad,
The learned regard it.
By Muirchertach with a goodly man's renown,
By Eogan's grandson.[140]

In the next year a further battle of Cell Osnaide[141] in Magh Fea[142] was fought where Aengus king of Munster with his wife Eithne the hateful[143] were also killed.[144] He was helped in this battle by Eochaidh, of the Ui Bairrche, brother of King Duach and also by Ailill and Illan sons of Dunlaing.. "By the plain of Meath it was lost and won", recorded Cenn Faelad a renowned poet of Ireland.[145] These battles gave the clan Niall the high

---

[138] Irish and Scottish Annals. First four lines attributed to *Beg Mac De*, sixth century Prophet.

[139] Possibly contraction of Magh Raighne – plain of the host? Or alternatively Grain?

[140] Book of Leinster poem by Flann Mainistrech, so mid eleventh century.

[141] Church of the deer/cattle?

[142] The plain of the Barrow in Co. Carlow

[143] Because she ate children. See The Expulsion of the Desi.

[144] Irish and Scottish Annals

kingship of Ireland at Tara under Lugaid and Mac Erca became king of Ailech[146] in 490.[147]

Grianan an Ailaech.

What is this mighty ring of stone

Set on a narrow neck of land

With seas to either hand?

'Tis the Grianan an Aileach

Home to the northern Ui Neill

And rival of Tara, herself!

Who made this ring of rocks

With gates to enter and leave

And stairways to climb?

---

[145] 7thC Irish poet who fought and was injured in the battle of Magh Rath and died in 679.

[146] Phases of Irish History by Eion MacNeill, Dublin 1920. Ailech – 'rock', referring to the rock citadel of the Kings of Ailech (genitive) and then to the land of Ailech. In old Irish genitive 'Alo' 'Aloo' See. A Grammar of Old Irish. Rudolf Thurneysen, D. A. Binchy, Dublin Institute for Advanced Studies, 1946 – "*ail 'rock', gen. alo (i-stem), also makes a gen. Ailech"*. Hence the 8th century scribe who wrote 'Rex Aloo' in the headings of Muircu's Life of Patrick probably meant that Coroticus was the king of Ailech in Donegal not king of Dumbarton. See Jackson and Dumville for discussions on Rex Aloo, Alo, Ail. An early form 'Ailgi' comes from the seventh century Terachan's Life of Patrick. Petrie described a circular ring of ten stones laid horizontally outside the main structure on a tumulus forming a stone platform or table, now unfortunately and very disappointingly, the round table is broken in pieces and probably buried.

[147] Flann Mainistrech in the book of Leinster states that Mac Erca was king of Ailech for 44 years. Counting back from 534 this gives a date of 490. *"Twice twenty reigned great Murchertach Mac Erca, chief of slaves, and four years for certain"*. Cenél Eoghan did not gain possession of the Grianan of Ailech until the late eighth century having defeated the Cenél Conaill in 789. Mac Erca would have been king of the territory known as Ailech, as apposed to the Grianan. He is usually associated with a fortress called Cletech on the Boyne and I wonder if this is a remembering of a fortress at Cloitech, modern Clady, As Cloitech sits on the river Finn, meaning 'white' and the Boyne also has a similar meaning – 'white Cow' the association has potential. Ibid Lacey for full details.

Some will say 'twas built by the hand

Of no less than The Dagda, himself

Atop the ruin of an ancient earthen fort.

Why is it here on this high point

Where the wind blows constant

And the rain seldom falls?

Look around, out from the wall

Five counties of Donegal you see

And the waters to each side.

And what purpose does it serve

Sitting atop the barren rocks

Between Donegal and the rest of Eire?

'Twas set to protect this far northern cape

And guard it safe from all intruders.

Who would take the kine and women of Ui Neill.[148]

During these years Muircertach married Duinsech[149], daughter of Duach Tengumha king of Munster and had three children – Fergus, Domnall [150] and Baedan[151]. Duach his father in law had

---

[148] Metrical Dindshenchas. http://www.ancienttexts.org/library/celtic/ctexts/d09.html

[149] 'Brunette', 'brown-haired girl'. 'The Virgin St. Duinsech and Her Three Ulster Churches near Strangford Lough, County Down', Centre for Irish and Celtic Studies, University of Ulster at Coleraine A. J. Hughes, Celtica 23, 1999. Welsh equivalent would be Gwinau-verch. Welsh Lexicon.

[150] Banshenchus, *Lore of Women*, notes sons as Eochu Find and Domnall the tall but this is in error as Eochid Find was a son of Domnal.. Books of Leinster, Lecan, Ui Maine, Ballymote; TCD H 3.17; N[r] VII Kilbride Coll.; Brussels MS 2542.

[151] This is interesting as it is pronounced like *Badon* and indeed in Scotland there are descendents of one *Baedan* who gave his name to a territory called in various sources Kinelbathyn, Kinelvadon or Kinelbadon, later contracted to Cenalbin, now Morvern in Argyle. Kinel meaning 'people or tribe of.' See The Life of St Columba of Hy by

shown Patrick respect when a young boy and so had been blessed by him and Patrick had attended his inauguration as King[152]. Baedan, Muircertach's son, was the father of Colman Rimid whose daughter Fina married Oswiu, King of the Saxons and their son was Aldfrid king of the Northumbrian Saxons [153].

In 499[154] the brother of King Duach, Eochaidh Tirmcharna, fell out of favour with Duach and so he was exiled and then sought the protection of Muircertach who was persuaded to give that protection by his wife Duinsech as Eochaidh was her foster father[155]. Unfortunately, Duach was able to capture and imprison Eochaide, which compelled Muircertach to war against his father in law. A series of battles were fought to settle the matter culminating in the battle of Seghais[156] near the Boyle river in which Duach was killed.

The battle of Seghais

A certain woman caused it;

Red blood was brought over lances

Adamnan. By William Reeves, Irish Archaeological and Celtic Society 1857. . The Spanish attributed an historical sixth century princess called Baddo/Badon with Arthur as his daughter – see Miscellaneous Tracts Vol.II by Michael Geddes circa 1714, P.62.

[152] G.Keating, History of Ireland, pg.29

[153] Aldfrith of Northumbria and the Irish Genealogies. Colin Ireland, Celtica 22, 1990. King 685-705

[154] McCarthy places it at 500 and the following battle of Inde Mor in 502 and the death of Fergus in 501 but this would spoil the chronology where Mac Erca is in Alba two years before killing Loarn.

[155] Annals of the Four Masters.

[156] Possibly meaning 'woods'. Segais - a magical well surrounded by hazel trees that is said to be the source of the Shannon and Boyne rivers. Compare to Arthurs *battle of the woods* in Celidon.

By Duinsech, daughter of Duach.

The battle of Delg[157], and battle of Mucremhe[158],

And the battle of Tuaim Drubha[159],

With the battle of Seghais, wherein fell Duach Tengumha[160].

And the battle of Seghais where Dui Tengumha fell,

It was won by Muirchertach the gentle,

It caused great wailing.[161]

This was followed by the battle of Inde Mor[162] in the year 500 when Muircertach fought the Leinstermen who were defeated and Illan son of Dunlaing was killed.

And the battle of Inde over Illan,

In which a brave man was slain;

Men raged in the strife against the hero of the Lagin.[163]

Muircertach's actions had now drawn the displeasure of the church and some holy poets called Crossans[164] lampooned him in

---

[157] Thorn or nail, possibly referring therefore to the Cross and crucifixion of Christ.

[158] Stout pig /boar??

[159] Fort of the ridge? Ridge/hill of death? The other word in Goidelic for *death and destruction* is `bath'.

[160] Chronicon Scotorum. Tengumha – *Bronze Tongue or sweet tongue.*

[161] Book of Leinster. Flann Mainistrech poem.

[162] Great paddock?

[163] The Book of Leinster. Flann Mainistrech poem. Lagin, modern Leinster.

[164] Crossans or Cross bearers were poets, whose principal office was to compose funeral dirges or family panegyrics, but who frequently degenerated into satirists

verse for his rather discrediting actions. In a fit of pique Muircertach murdered the holy Crossans and for these murders he was exiled from Ireland to Alba and to the court of King Loarn his maternal grandfather in Argyll. However this did not stop his tyrannical ways and after two years in Alba he murdered King Loarn by setting him aflame[165]. Loarn was buried in Iona[166]. After this Loarn's brother Fergus became King. It is said that Muircertach was in possession of the Lia Fáil, the Stone of Destiny[167] and in recompense for the murder of Loarn he allowed the stone to be taken to Fergus in Alba for his coronation where it remained for the coronation of future kings of Scotland and then England.

The Scotic nation,

Noble the race,

Unless the prophecy be false,

Ought to obtain dominion,

Where they shall find the Lia Fáil.[168]

---

against those who had incurred Church censure, which brought them into conflict with lawless chieftains. The Irish Version of the Historia Brittonum of Nennius, James Henthorn Todd, Algernon Herbert 1848. Being satarised like this was akin to being excommunicated and could result in the forfeiture of honour price and kingship. See Irish Kings and High Kings, Francis J. Byrne, Four Courts Press 2001. pg.15.

[165] Aided Muirchertaig Meic Erca — "The Death of Muirchertach mac Erca. Dublin, Trinity College, MS H 2.16 (cat. 1318) Yellow Book of Lecan and Dublin, Trinity College, MS H 2.7 (cat. 1928)

[166] Pictish Sourcebook By J. M. P. Calise, Greenwood Press 2002. Regnal Lists D, F1,F, I, K..

[167] Keating, History of Ireland, P.207 citing Hector Boetius. . I am uncertain as to their original sources.

[168] Ibid.P.207. Also see Skene, 'Celtic Scotland', Edinburgh, 1890.

Fergus however did not live long dying at the hands of his brother[169] in about 502 possibly following the struggles with Mac Erca for the return of the Lia Fáil. One Domangart Réti (of Riatai) son of Fergus is then said to have reigned in Argyll, again only for a short time until around 506 when he retired to the church and soon died[170] His son Comgall took the regency. His reign was a long and peaceful one with no battles after which his brother Gabran took the regency.[171]

For the murder of Loarn, Muircertach was exiled from Alba by Fergus's men and so went to the Britons of Strathclyde under the protection of their king Lugaid from whom he learned all the science of weapons and warfare[172]. It then came to the time when Muircertach would have his weapons consecrated and so his maternal uncle, Bishop Cairnech, was called to do his duty in this respect. He travelled to the British court and when he saw how powerful Muircertach had become he decided on a plan to punish his brother Lugaid for building his fort in the precinct of his monastery. He said to Muircertach "Thou shalt be king of Ireland and of Britain for ever, and shalt go to heaven after, provided thou canst but prevent Lugaide from exercising his power against the Church". Muircertach later approached King Lugaid and said

---

[169] Chronicles of the Picts, Chronicles of the Scots. William F Skene, 1867, p.309. However this may refer to Fergus Bec instead.

[170] Annals Of Ulster : 'Domangart Mac Nissi of Réte retired into religion in his 35th year'.

[171] Duan Albanach mentions Comgells lack of battles. Gabran reigned from 537 which again is interesting as this is the time when Arthur is said to have died.

[172] Banshenchus call him " Murchertach, (of) the mighty weapon, son of Erc". C. Dobbs, Maighreád "The Ban-shenchus". Revue Celtique. vol. 47-49

"Build not thine city in the precincts of Cairnech the Bishop" but Lugaid said in reply "I think more of the power of that pet wild fawn he has, than of his power, or of the power of the lord God whom he adores." Muircertach related these words to Cairnech who flew into a great rage and proclaimed "My prayer to my Lord, to my God, let that very fawn be the cause of his death, and by thy hand O Mac Erca!" Cairnech then commanded Muircertach to destroy his brother and Mac Erca agreed to the task.

He approached Lugaid as the king was out with his assembly in the grounds of his fort. God then worked a miracle for Cairnech, for he sent a wild fawn from the mountainside into the assembly and the whole host of nobles decided to chase it except Lugaid and his women. Mac Erca said to Lugaid "If you had been just my lord, towards your cleric, it is certain that it would have given you increased happiness to have worn the royal robe" and with that Muircertach thrust his spear right through the kings body killing him instantly[173]. He then cut off the head and took it to Cairnech and proclaimed, "lo, here is thy brothers head for thee O Cairnech". Cairnech said "leave me the bone, eat thou the marrow and every third coarb shall be thine for ever, here in Britain and in Ireland". Others say that a lightning bolt killed Lugaide in the year 506 for denying the saint[174]; either way,

---

[173] Baile Chuind Chétchathaig, circa 670 mentions after Lugaid "A glorious man upon him, Mac Ercene"

[174] Chronicon Scottorum, 'Death of Lugaide, son of Laeghaire, King of Temhair, in Achadh Farcha. He was struck on the head with lightning from heaven, for denying the Saint'. The Saint herein referred to is usually taken to be St.Patrick as mentioned in the

Muircertach now had to establish his rule over the Britons of Strathclyde and Alba with the help of Cairnech. Muircertach immediately moved against the nobility of the land taking hostages to guarantee allegiance and probably brought Comgall, King of Argyll under his authority without a fight[175]. With the death of Lugaid, he now pursued his widowed wife who was the daughter of the king of the Franks[176]. After many battles with the Franks he won her and then produced the children – Constantine[177], Gaedhal-Ficht[178] (from whom are descended the kings of Britain, and the kings of Cornwall); Nellenn and Scannal[179]. He ruled together with Cairnech for seven years[180] in which time he

---

Annals of the Four Masters but this is a very late compilation of the seventeenth century. The entry in the CS therefore is earlier. Interesting then that in this tale the 'Saint' is Cairnech and the person who struck him was Mac Erca. It seems too coincidental to have two Lughaidh's die at practically the same time so I have equated them. I would suggest that Lugaidh son of Logaire was adopted into Irish genealogies and was actually a king of the Britons, later known as Lew who may have held some territory in Ireland as well as in Strathclyde. He also appears to have been Christian having no Feis Temro mentioned. His absence of battles in the annals has always puzzled commentators as well, as Lacey, ibid, mentions.

[175] The very name in its earliest form by Adamnan – Comgell, means to 'pledge or promise'.

[176] 'rig francg' quite an early spelling also used by Adamnan in the late C7th and in Cormac's Glossaries in the C9th

[177] Appears to be the same Constantine of Gildas and Geoffrey of Monmouth! Relates that Constantine was a king of Britain as were his descendents. Gildas's Damnonia could mean either Dumnonia or possibly Damnonia in the far north. Interestingly Clovis was called the 'new Constantine' at his late baptism by Gregory of Tours. Dudley Mac Firbis quotes this legend of Constantine et al in his C17th work saying it came from "a very ancient book" and that the book said "nothing more about him (Mac Erca) than that" so unlikely it was from the tale of St Cairnech.

[178] Gaedhal – Irish, Ficht – Pict. Appears to mean the Cornish kings were descended from Irish and Briton (Picts) mix which could indeed be true.

[179] Descendants in Ireland.

[180] Welsh Triads appear to reflect this - The Three Red Ravagers : "..Arthur was his name. For a year neither grass nor plants used to spring up where one of the three would walk; but where Arthur went, not for seven years. " In Goidelic 'Erc' can also

brought the Britons, Saxons, Picts, Irish[181], Orkneys and Denmark under his sway. Muircertach later uttered these words concerning his victories:

My wrath has ended here,

Since I came over sea to Erin,

I remember the number of years,

I have never seen a day, lasting the fame,

Without a hero's head and a triumph over him.

I was eleven years without finding domain.

Until then, there was no night

without a head of Leinster or Munster.

I was myself twenty years

in the kingdom of Eogan, son of Niall;

I had every night without a doubt a head

Of Ulster and Connaught.

I was twenty-five years without fail

in the kingship of Ireland.

There was no night so far

Without the slaying of someone in Ireland.

Two years I was east in Alba,

I have killed my grandsire,

---

mean 'red'.

[181] Gerald Of Wales (12th Century) asserts that Arthur had many kings of the Irish `tributarie to him'. James A. Knapp 'Illustrating the Past in Early Modern England: The Representation of History in Printed Books', Ashgate Publishing; illustrated edition, 2003. Pg.222. Also see Culhwch and Olwen where the Irish kings and Saints submit to Arthur, offering victuals and blessings, – The Mabinogian, Gwyn Jones, Thomas Jones, Dragons Dream B.V. 1982, p.122.

I have brought a host there into troubles,

By my deeds Loarn fell.

Two years I was afterwards

In kingship over Danes,

There has been no night there at

Without the heads of two on stakes.

Here is my true confession

In the presence of the king of kings.

I have been much of my days without weakness,

And I have not been near death.[182]

With the King of the Franks[183] defeated and dead by 511 Cairnech called a synod of Bishops[184] at Tours of Martin where attended three hundred and thirty seven bishops under the authority of the Pope to cast out every heresy and to reduce every country to the discipline of the Church. Cairnech then made a pilgrimage to Léon[185] in honour of Muiredach and Muircertach. After this, he went to the Britons of Cornwall and founded a city he built underground[186]. Cairnech is said to have been in Ireland before Muircertach so that he was the first bishop of the Clan-

---

[182] From 'Aided Muircertach Mac Erca,' The Death of Muircertach Mac Erca.

[183] The only 'King of the Franks' at this time would have been Clovis himself who did indeed die around this time, between 511-513!

[184] Clovis had called a synod of Bishops to Orleans shortly before his death in 511 or 513. Gregory of Tours, 'History of the Franks'.

[185] 'Lien' in M. Probably Léon in Brittany or Lyon in Frankia. I suggest Leon in Brittany which had an early Bishopric as from there to Cornwall is only a short hop. But Orleans could even be meant.

[186] Very similar to story of St Carranog who built a city of the dead in Cornwall.

Niall and of Tara and he was the first martyr and the first monk of Ireland, and the first Judge of the men of Ireland.

Cinel Eogain, nobler than the kindred of Tara,
With fingers decked with many rings, with the beauty of their hair,
They are the noblest array in Erin, the assembly of Ailech;
They are the best that a retinue surrounds in their homes in the west.
Seventeen High Kings from them, of the line of Eoghan, ruled over Erin:
Their foreign levies would contend for their rights in the world,
By them are hostages taken from every land I traverse;
Through them, all men are thriving in Erin.[187]

The Franks and Saxons then rose up again to challenge Muircertach but due to his power and strength, he defeated them both and all their cities and surrounding countries after a long campaign. This all took place during a period of seven years where Muircertach and Cairnech ruled jointly. Then, in around 513[188] he took his large fleet of ships and landed in Ireland at Fan-na-long[189] where he then defeated any opposition from the Irish kings and was declared High King of all Ireland. Mac Erca took their sovereignty by right forever, for himself and for his descendants.

---

[187]From the Metrical Dindshenchas.
http://www.ucc.ie/celt/published/T106500D/text025.html

[188] McCarthy reconciles this to 510. The usual time given for the interregnum before Muircertach's High Kingship is five years but in this story it is seven meaning we must date it to 513 agreeing as it does with the AU entry.

[189] 'The drawing up in his ships'. M implies the meaning is that the ships were burnt but this doesn't appear to be correct.

He was thirty years in Britain, no lie,

In that time he took possession

Of the Saxon and Briton hosts.

Ten years after that,

They assembled in a severe attack;

The Saxons and the Britons without grief,

Their assembly aimed towards Ireland.[190]

The destruction of sixty kings

And one hundred prosperous rulers

By the charm and power of Mac Erca,

He took revenge for his father.

The speckled man[191] and undefeated hero of battle,

The bright and radiant warrior of the whole of Europe.[192]

In the year 520 Muircertach sent messengers to demand the Boru or cow tribute from the Leinstermen as normal but this time it was refused and battle offered instead[193]. He therefore assembled the men of Northern Ireland[194] and the nobles of the race of Conall Earrbreagh, the son of Niall. The Leinstermen

---

[190] Aided Muircertach Mac Erca.

[191] Pun on his name Erca, which can also mean *speckled*. eDill.

[192] By Flann Mainistrech from the Book of Leinster (7.10 and 11). Some of these lines might have been taken by Flann from an earlier poem possibly about Mael Umai.

[193] George Petrie, 'On the history and antiquities of Tara Hill', *Transactions of the Royal Irish Academy* 18 (1839), 25–232: 25, relates this story of the demand for the Boru.

[194] Leath-Cuinn, meaning 'Conn's half', the northern half of Ireland where Conn's descendants ruled particularly from Ailech in Tir Conell, *the Land of Conn*, later Donegal.

advanced to Bregia to challenge Muircertach and Colga, son of Cloite, king of Airghialla. There in Bregia the battle of Detnae was fought between them, in which were slain Ardgal, the son of Conall Creamhthainne, and Colga, King of Airghialla. The Leinstermen were defeated in this battle and others, so that Muircertach raised the tribute without a battle afterwards. St. Columba was born this year.

Ardgal son of Conall of the forays,

Seven years over fielded Meath ;

A draught from death's well he drank

In the battle of Detna with the Lagin.[195]

For ten long years there was peace in Ireland, Britain and Gaul and the tribute was paid to Muircertach but then by 529 the men of Leinster sought once more for an end to tribute and called their people to war. Mac Erca answered the challenge. First was fought the battles of Cenn Eich[196] and then Ath Sighe[197] at Cerb on the Boyne in which Muircertach was victorius. Sighe son of Dian died in this battle, his daughter would one day seek revenge. Bishop Cairnech was heard to prophesize:

I am fearful of the woman,

Around whom many storms shall move,

---

[195] Book of Leinster poem by Flann Mainistrech.

[196] Horse Head, meaning the Hill of the Horse? Kinneigh on borders of Kildare and Wicklow. *Keeting,* History of Ireland

[197] Ford of Victory. In myth Sighe father of Sin (Sheen)

For the man who shall be burned in fire

On the side of Cletty wine shall drown.

Sin is the woman who kills thee,

O, son of Erca, as I see.

The men of Connaught now joined with those of Leinster in the revolt and in March 531 Muircertach fought the battle of Ebhlinn[198] and further battles in one famous year against these rebels. In all he was victorius.

The battle of Cenn-eich; the battle of Almhaine[199],

It was an illustrious, famous period,

The devastation of the Cliachs; the battle of Aidhne[200];

And the battle of Magh Ailbhe.[201]

The bitter battle of Sliab[202] Ebhlinn

Over the nobles of Munster

And over Echaid Sremm,

Where many heads of heroes were left.[203]

The king Mac Erc

Returned to the side of the descendants of Niall.

---

[198] Flowing pool/river? Similar to Arthurs last battle 'Camlann' –crooked pool.

[199] Old Irish Almu, 'Knee cap', topographical description, the hill of Allen in Leinster. *Keeting*, History of Ireland

[200] The old place? In the south of Co. Galway.

[201] In Kildare, *Keeting*, History of Ireland.

[202] Sliab = moor in this case rather than mountain. eDill.

[203] These four lines from Book of Leinster poem by Flann Mainistrech.

Blood reached the girdle of the plain.

The exterior territories were enriched.

Seventeen times nine chariots he brought

And long shall it be remembered.

He bore away the hostages of the Ui-Niell

With the hostages of the plain of Munster. [204]

Full twenty battles and two

Clearness of record hath ascertained.

Great Muirchertach Mac Erca won without sorrow.[205]

These were Mac Erca's greatest victories ensuring tribute, honour and peace for the rest of his life.

Muircertach then called a feast at Dun Turleim to hear the petitions of the O'Neill clans for the right to the governance of Ireland after him. He gave precedence of petition to O Cuinne[206] the Active, son of Ailill, son of Eoghan, son of Niall Naoighiallach and to his descendants after him, and moreover that they should be buried in every burial place of the kings of Ireland in preference to every other line descended from Eoghan,

---

[204] Attributed to the 7thC poet Ceanfaeladh in the Annals of the Four Masters. Also cited by George Petrie, 'On the history and antiquities of Tara Hill.' The Bodleian Dindshenchas however has a version of this said to have been sung by Bishop Mel, who died circa 489 which is obviously wrongly attributed.

[205] Book of Leinster poem by Flann Mainistrech and obviously a great exaggeration as it was more like twelve as discussed above.

[206] O Cuinne is of course just the old name of the O'Neills from Moccu or Ui Conn – descendants of Conn. This snippet of a tale seems to be relating a prophecy of the domination of the O'Neills in the Irish Kingship following Mac Erca. Also much more, to be discussed later.

because it was Cuinne who went to the Munster war on behalf of Muircertach[207].

It is said of Mac Erca, of the great attacks, that he was no heathen, that he ruled without exercising undue power and without treachery; that he subdued powerful armies and was one of two hereditary champions of his time the other being the emperor Justinian[208]. Some say that Muircertach died naturally in his bed[209] but other traditions say his death was a violent one; and then the power and strength of Britain was destroyed after him.[210]

---

[207] "Ceart Ui Neill." trans. and ed. by Myles Dillon. Studia Celtica. Volume 1. Cardiff: UWP. (Studia Celtica, By University of Wales Board of Celtic Studies Published by University of Wales Press., 1966, Item notes: v.1-5 1969-1970, pp 1-18.)

[208] Ibid Imarcaigh sund ar gach saí – P. J. Smith, University of Ulster: "Great Muirchertach mac Earca is selected on account of his great attacks, without exercising undue power, without any treachery from him as high-king of all Ireland....during the reign of great Muircheartach who subdued powerful armies....Justin [I] was his successor in the East in the time of spirited Muircheartach; the two hereditary champions of authority, their contemporaneous kingships were harmonious...in the time of the king, he was shrewd without exercising undue power....The death of Muircheartach son of Earc about that time, he was no heathen.." http://www.ucc.ie/celt/Imarcaigh.pdf

[209] Keeting, History of Ireland

[210] ..'and the power and strength of Britain was destroyed after him'... from 'Of the Miracles of Cairnech Here'. The last sentence.

The Violent Death of Muircertach mac Erca.[211]

1. Muircertach son of Muiredach, son of Eoghan, King of Ireland, was in the palace of Cletech[212], on the bank of Boyne of the Brug with his wife, Duinsech daughter of Duach brazen tongue King of Connacht. Muircertach came forth one day to hunt on the border of the Brug, and his hunting companions left him alone on his hunting mound.

2. He had not been there long when he saw a solitary damsel beautifully formed, fair-headed, bright-skinned, with a green mantle about her, sitting near him on the turf mound; and it seemed to him that of womankind he had never seen her equal in beauty and refinement. All his body and his nature filled with love for her, for gazing at her it seemed to him that he would give the whole of Ireland for one night's loan of her, so utterly did he love her at first sight. He welcomed her as if she was known to him, and he asked tidings of her.

---

[211] Based on translation by Whitley Stokes, edited and updated by myself and verse translations with help of the French translation, Le Mort De Muirchertach, Fils De Erc, J Guyonvarc'h, Annales. Économies, Sociétés, Civilisations, Année 1983, Volume 38, Numéro 5 pp. 985 – 1015 and with help from the scholars of the Irish L discussion list. Also the use of Lil Nic Donnchadha's vocabulary list in Aided was most helpful.

[212] A 14th/15th Century reference indicates that it lay near the Sid in Broga (Newgrange), opposite Knowth, Co. Meath. Possibly the current location of Rossnaree House. Dindshenchas describe it as 'the top of all houses in Erin' – 'Newgrange and the Bend of the Boyne', Geraldine Stout, 2002 pg.68

3. "I will tell you," she said. "I am the darling of Muircertach Mac Erca, King of Erin, and to seek him I came here." That seemed good to Muircertach, and he said to her, "Do you know me, O damsel?" "I do," she answered; "for skilled am I in places more secret than this, and known to me are you and the other men of Erin." "Will you come with me, O damsel?" said Muircertach. "I would go," she answered, "provided my reward be good." I will give you power over me, O damsel," said Muircertach. "Your word for this!" rejoined the damsel and he gave it at once and she sang this song:

His power is not; his person is ready,
But for the teachings of the clerics,
But for the mildness of the day,
By no means would I have come here.

Do not proceed to the will of the clerics
Until your woman is ready.
Do not yourself go through the clerics,
Do not do anything for them.

Do not take the sharp chides of the Clerics
I am the illustrious woman of soft voice,
Every person is better for it having fed of me.
Be not obedient to those sulphurous Clerics.

Muircertach:

O woman, do not say this.

Do not rebuke the people of the faith,

The Clerics who believe in Chris.

There is no one more skilful than they.

4. "I will give you a hundred of every herd, and a hundred drinking-horns, and a hundred cups, and a hundred rings of gold, and a feast every other night in the house of Cletech." "No," said the damsel; "not so shall it be. What I want is that my name must never be uttered by you, and Duinsech, the mother of your children, must not be in my sight, and clerics must never enter the house that I am in." "All this you shall have," said the king, "for I pledged you my word; but it would be easier for me to give you half of Ireland. And tell me truly;" said the king, "what is your name, so that we may avoid it by not uttering it." And she said, "Sigh, Sough, Sin (Storm), Rough Wind, Winter☐ Night, Cry, Wail, Groan." So then, he uttered this lay:

Tell me your name, O damsel,

You most beloved, star-bright lady,

You who parts me from my family,

Don't hide it from me by withholding it.[213]

---

[213] Thanks to Sean O'Connor and Neil McLeod of the Irish Language mailing list for help with this line.

Sin:

Sigh, Roaring, Storm without reproach

Rough wind and winter nights,

Tears, Lament, the silent Wail

And the sound of the weeping cow.

M:

I will give you a hundred heads

Oh damsel without error,

If you would allow me oh maiden to utter your name,

To be saying each, one at a time.

Sin:

What good would it be to suffer wounds?

Oh king of Ireland, ultimate ruler.

You will die if you say them oh king,

Your strength will come to nothing.

M:

To be injured would not be pleasant at this time

Oh damsel of brightness to mine eyes.

 Alas this is indeed too true,

 Sigh, Roar and Storm.

Sin:

You cannot speak this without weakness,

It would be an easy way to your early death,

And you would not be able to come to

The mother of your children, Duinsech.

M:

I will happily to do your will,

Let your mind not be anxious.

Do not say any more words of foreboding,

I will not utter or speak [your names].

5. Each of these things was promised to her, and thus he pledged himself. Then they went together to the house of Cletech.

Good was the arrangement of that house,

Good were its household and staff,

And all the nobles of the clan Niall,

Cheerfully and spiritedly, gaily and gladly,

Consuming the tribute and wealth of every province

In the trophy-decorated house of Cletech.

Above the brink of the salmon-filled Boyne,

Ever lovely above the green topped Brug.[214]

And give thou testimony as to this house," said the king. So she said:

---

[214] Brug – a plain.

Never has been built by a king above the waves

A house like thy home above the Boyne,

It will never be out done,

Until the final forces of doomsday.

Cletech the choicest home of Fodla[215]

It is known far and wide

From Thoraid to Carnd Ui Neit[216]

Before it there is no finer, no doubt.

The Clann of Eoghan in that house,

The high race of Niall, who are not in need,

No family is there better amongst

The countries of Alban and Ireland.

O thou, Muirchertaig, without treason,

There was never a hero who came against you

That would come another day.

O grandson of Eoghan, no one like you.

She is suitable for you, no doubt,

Duinsech, daughter of the king of Connacht.

---

[215] Early name of Donegal or northern Ireland, related to Fochla meaning the North.

[216] From one end of Ireland to the next. Carnd Ui Neit is Mizen Head at extreme west of Ireland. Thoraid is probably Tory Island, at the northeast tip, now called Toraigh ('Thur-ri' sorrowful head?)

She is desirable of form and of beautiful complexion.
There is no better wife around us.

7. "What shall be done here now?" demanded the damsel. "That which you desire," replied Muircertach. "If so," said Sin, "let Duinsech and her children leave the house, and let a man of every craft and art in Ireland come with his wife into the drinking-hall." Thus it was done, and each began praising his own craft and art, and a stave was made by every craftsman and artist who was therein:

Pleasant, pleasant the noble realm
Of Erin's land, great is its rank,
It is customary to receive tributes
In the lovely house of Cleitech.

Pleasant, pleasant is the kingdom of the Queen
Pleasant and gentle are its maledictions
Finding good work is easy,
To dance is to have pleasure.

Pleasant, pleasant is the principate,
The King of Ireland holds Royal power,
Although Ireland is close to us,
What man would not find it pleasant?

Pleasant, pleasant is its agriculture,

To the man who lives in the country,

Lots of cattle and suitable work,

Without poverty, it is agreeable.

Pleasant, pleasant the music undoubtedly is,

Musicians with noble qualities,

Has anyone sung more melodiously?

It is nice to hear them always.

Pleasant, pleasant is the art of forging,

The people who practice without hindrance,

For the good of the people and the church,

This power is not unpleasant.

Pleasant, pleasant, be lovely metal work,

To all those who practice together,

There are many servants for us,

It is for us a delightful hill.

Pleasant, pleasant is the valour,

Of Mac Erca of great strength,

In the house of Cleitech of diligent work,

Who would not find this fortress agreeable?

Pleasant, pleasant is every difficult art,

Now in the land of Ireland,

That everyone uses diligently,

Among the nobles, it is pleasing.

8. When the drinking was ended Sin said to Muircertach, "It is time now to leave the house to me, as hath been promised." Then she put the Clan of Niall, and Duinsech with her children, forth out of Cletech; and this is their number, both men and women, two equally great and gallant battalions.

9. Duinsech went with her children from Cletech to Tuilen[217], to seek her confessor the holy bishop Cairnech. When she got to Cairnech she uttered these words:

O cleric, bless my body,

I am afraid of death to-night,

A woman of the Síd appeared to me.

I was powerless against her.

Cairnech:

O woman, your fate will be good

You shall have heaven, no lie

The journey that you have undertaken,

You do not have to make again.

---

[217] Dulane in Co. Meath.

Duinsech:

Arise and go there yourself O Cleric

To the children of Eogan and Conall,

As we are under a yoke together

We are humbled on the hill.

Cairnech:

Later you will go to Oenach Reil,

O Duinsech of good virtue,

It is you that will forever,

Prevail over that ancient tree of the fortress.

Duinsech:

I thank the son of Mary,

And the king who sees everything,

That you believe in me,

I thank you, O Cleric.

10. Thereafter Cairnech came to the descendents of Eogan and Conall, and they went back together to Cletech, but Sin would not let them near the fortress. At this act the Clan of Niall were dis□tressed and mournful. Then Cairnech was greatly angered, and he cursed the house, and made a grave for the king, and said, "He whose grave this is hath finished; and truly it is an end to his realm and his princedom!" And he went to the top of the grave, and said:

The mound of these bells forever,
Henceforward everyone will know,
The grave of the champion Mac Erca:
Not slack have been his journeys.
A curse upon this hill,
On Cletech with hundreds of troops!
May neither its corn nor its milk be good,
May it be full of hatred and evil plight!
May neither king nor prince be in it,
May no one come out of it victoriously!
During my day I shall remember
The King of Erin's grave in the mound.

11. So then Cairnech cursed the fortress and blessed a place therein, and then he came forth in grief and sorrow. And the Clan of Niall said to him, "Bless us now, O cleric, that we may go to our own country, for we are not guilty in regards to you"

12. Cairnech blessed them and left a grant to them, namely, to the Clan Conall and the Clan Eogan, that whenever they had not the leadership or the kingship of Ireland, their power should be over every province around them; and that they should have the - succession of Ailech and Tara and Ulster; and that they should take no wage from any one, for this was their own inherent right, the kingship of Ireland. That they should be without fetter or

hostage, and that there should be decay upon the hostages if they absconded; and that they should gain victory in battle provided it was delivered for a just cause, and that they should have three standards, namely, the Cathach and the Bell of Patrick (i.e., of the Bequest), and the Misach of Cairnech, and that the grace of these reliquaries should be on any one of them against battle, as Cairnech left to them, saying:

My blessing on you till doomsday,
O Clan of Niall constantly,
Un-plundered are the lands of Mac Erca,
Your adventures will be famous.

Do not kill hostages oh glorious King.
Whether near or far,
Your nobility will want for nothing,
Your sovereignty will be endless.

Your descendants will never be overthrown,
They will never offer submission,
They will not refuse the challenge of combat,
They will never be without prosperity.

You carry out plundering across the land,
Because you are the High King,
Then will be destruction and no submission,

Unless to the king alone.

You possess hostages with strength of arms,
 But you are not repentant as the book teaches,
All will flee before you in battle,
Until the end times, nothing the like of it.

You have brothers of your own.
Whether near or far.
The legacy and inheritance of your battles,
Your deeds shall last for all time.

When you threaten, it shall not be gentle,
You will be feared in every land,
Everyone will hear of your good fortune,
In each country, you will be dreaded.

I speak of the truth that
When you shall die O' king,
I will say prayers from the book for you,
Moreover, the writing shall be in blood.

With the blood of the arm,
The death of your royal lineage,
Will be like gore and blood,
Between Loch Febail and the Sea.

My blessing on your country,
To your men of bright virtue,
Yours will be Ériu forever,
And you have my blessing.

Each of them then went to their own stronghold and their own good place.

13. Cairnech came on towards his monastery, and there met him great hosts, namely the descendants of Tadg son of Cian son of Ailill Olom. And they brought Cairnech with them to make their arrangement and their treaty with Muircertach Mac Erca; and when the king was told of this, he came forth from his stronghold and bade them welcome.

14. But when Muircertach espied the cleric with them, there came a great blush upon him, and he exclaimed, "Why have you come: to us, O cleric, after cursing us?" "I have come," he answered, "to make peace between the descendants of Tadg son of Cian and the descendants of Eogan Mac Neill." And Muircertach said to Cairnech:

Go, thou cleric, afar,
Be not near, against our will,
You have placed a curse

Over my royal grave.

Cairnech:

The reason I am here,

Ignoring the curse,

Is to seal the treaty

Between the tribes of Eoghan and Tadg.

For both the Gailenga and the Luigne,

And the Saitne Ciandacht are all in agreement.

The men of Ard Dealbna are of the same accord.

The descendents of Aeda Odba being exempt.

Your bloods have co joined,

With Mac Erca's of great strength,

And it has been written by me in the book,

This treaty with Clann Eoghan and the Gailenga.

Should anyone curse either party,

In this treaty of Sil Eoghan and Sil Tadg,

Be great injury inflicted upon them,

And great hurt be carried always.

If a bondsman kills another,

Such betrayal shall not be good,

His body shall be destroyed,

It will be as nothing.

This is your alliance here,
As granted by heaven in your honour,
I will preserve it in memory,
As I raise this vessel.

Then a treaty was made between them, and Cairnech mingled the blood of both of them in one vessel, and wrote how they had made the treaty then.

15. Then when the treaty had been made, and when Cairnech had blessed them all, and left shortness of life and hell to him who should knowingly infringe the treaty, he quitted them and returned to his monastery. And the king went to his stronghold, and those hosts with him, to guard against the Clan of Niall.

16. The king sat on his throne, and Sin sat on his right, and never on earth had there come a woman better than she in shape and appearance. The king looked on her, and sought knowledge and asked questions of her, for it seemed to him that she was a goddess of great power, and he asked her what was the power that she had. Like this he spoke and she answered:

Muircertach:
Tell me, you ready damsel,

Do you believe in the God of the clerics?

Or from whom you have sprung in this world?

Tell us your origin.

Sin:

I believe in the same true God

Helper of my body against death's attack;

You cannot work in this world a miracle

Of which I could not work its like.

I am the daughter of a man and a woman

Of the race of Adam and Eve;

I am fit for you here,

Let no regret seize you.

I could create a sun and a moon,

And radiant stars:

I could create men fiercely

Fighting in conflict.

I could make wine—no falsehood—

Of the Boyne, as I can obtain it,

And sheep of stones,

And swine of ferns.

I could make silver and gold

In the presence of the great hosts:

I could make famous men now for you.

17. "Work for us," said the king, "some of these great miracles." Then Sin went forth and arrayed two battalions equally great, equally strong, and equally gallant. It seemed to them that never came on earth two battalions that were bolder and more heroic than they, slaughtering and maiming and swiftly killing each other in the presence of every one.

18. "Do you see that?" said the damsel; "indeed my power is in no wise a fraud." "I see," said Muircertach, and he said:

I see two battalions bold and fair
On the plain in strife,
No one will believe that there is not
Battle and conflict here.
The brave battalions perform feats.
We will break them with our superior weapons,
We will not cease to smite their bodies,
It is not a displeasing battle.
Never was there such a conflict on earth,
With warlike men who were not worthy,
Never has come two battalions like these I see.

19. Then the king with his household came into the fortress. When they had been a while seeing the fighting, some of the water of the Boyne was brought to them, and the king told the damsel to make wine of it. The damsel then filled three casks

with water, and cast a spell upon them; and it seemed to the king and his household that never came on earth wine of better taste or strength. So of the fern she made fictitious swine of enchantment, and then she gave the wine and the swine to the host, and they partook of them until, as they supposed, they were sated. Furthermore, she promised that she would give them forever and forever the same amount; whereupon Muircertach said:

Hitherto never has come here
Food like the food ye see,
No end of wine as if it is wine
A feast worthy of a noble king.

Sin:
Sufficient for the men of Ireland,
Forever you have this ford.
The beer and wine has made you weak,
Evil is the fairy troop.

Mac Erca:
Bless this green and our strength,
Oh beautiful maiden of magic.
Good fortune to whom it reaches,
If the maiden does not lie.

20. So the descendants of Tadg son of Cian, when the partaking of the magical feast was ended, kept watch over the king that night. When he rose on the morrow he was as if he were in a decline, and so was everyone else who had partaken of the wine and the ficti☐tious magical flesh which Sin had arranged for that feast. And the king said:

O damsel, my strength has departed,
My final burial has almost come
After that night even though not injured,
I feel weak and languid.

Sin:
The wine you consumed, O King,
There is none that has been stronger.
It has consumed your wonderful body,
But it will do no harm to your soul.

M:
We two people are meant to be,
You and me O lovely woman,
You are the damsel chosen for me.

21. Then the king said to her, "Show us something of your art, O damsel!" "I will do so indeed," said she. They fared forth, that is, Muircertach and all the hosts that were with him. Then Sin made

of the stones blue men, and others with heads of goats; so that there were four great battalions under arms before him on the green of the Brug. Muircertach then seized his arms and his battle-dress and went among them like a swift, angry, mad bull, and forthwith took to slaughtering them and wounding them, and every man of them that be killed used to rise up after him at once. And thus he was killing them through the fair day till night. Though great were the rage and the wrath of the king, he was wearied thus, and he said:

I see a marvel on that side,
In the foaming waters of the river,
All those from the battalions I killed
Are alive with gory bodies.

Sin:
Your sovereignty has come to an end,
I cannot deny it O noble king,
For each of those that your hand has destroyed,
It is fitting that they are still alive.

It is the truth I tell,
I cannot conceal the host from you,
The blue men in battle and contention,
Are more powerful than the great son.

Mac Erca:

I say that I do not hack the heather,

This is not the combat of a strong champion.

I have defeated many hundreds of armies,

By the courageous struggles of my red sword.

Sin:

To the Cleric who helped you,

Let him write about this brave struggle,

About the multitude who fell miserably,

The blue men with heads of goats.

Mac Erca:

I will deliver proper combat.

So do not revile the cleric.

My memory is recovering now,

I can see the battle.

22. So when the king was weary from fighting and smiting the hosts, he came sadly into the fortress, and Sin gave him magical wine and magical pig's flesh. And he and his household partook of them, and at the end he slept heavily until morning, and when rising on the morrow be had neither strength nor vigour. And he said:

I am without strength, thou gentle lady,

Even if my fortress were threatened with destruction,

I would be unable to raise my right arm in its defence,

I would be neglecting my duty, which would not be good.

Sin:

The holy Cleric has spoken,

Your death has nearly come,

He will help you again,

Do not leave with ignorance.

Mac Erca:

It is good to recall completely,

What now the lovely maiden brings.

And today even in oppression,

I will not give up someone like you.

23. As they were saying this, they heard the heavy shout of the hosts and the multitudes, calling Muircertach forth and challenging him to battle. Then in his presence in the Brug were two battalions equally great, to wit, blue men in one of the two and headless men in the other. Muircertach was enraged at the challenge of the hosts, and he rose up suddenly, but fell exhausted on the floor, and uttered this lay:

A heavy shout, a noise which hosts make,

A battalion of blue men to the north of us,

Headless men who begin battle

In the glen to the south of us.

Weak is my strength: unto a host,

'Twas many times that I have brought victory;

Great was the host, stark their division,

Rude their name, rough their shout.

24. Then he went into the Brug and charged through the hosts, and took to slaughtering and maiming them long through the day. There came Sin to them and gave Muircertach kingship over them, and he rested from battling. And then the king fared forth to Cletech, and Sin formed two great battalions between him and the fortress. When he saw them he charged through them and began to do battle against them.

25. Now when he was delivering that battle, then Cairnech sent Masan and Casan and Cridan to seek him, so that he might have God's assistance, for the high saint knew of the oppression be suffered at that time. The clerics met him in the Brug, while he was hacking the stones and the sods and the stalks; and one of the clerics spoke and Muircertach answered:

Cleric.

Why do you fell the stones,

O Muircertach, without reason?

We are sad that you are weak,

According to the will of an idolater working magic.

Mac Erca:

The cleric who attacked me,

I came into conflict with him:

I know not furthermore

That the stones are not alive.

Cleric.

Put Christ's mysterious cross

Now over thine eyes:

Abate for a time thy furies:

For what reason do you fell the stones?

26. Then the soldier's royal wrath ceased and his senses came to him, and he put the sign of the Cross over his face, and then he saw nothing there save the stones and sods of the earth. Then he asked tidings of the clerics, and said, "Why do you come?" "We came," they answered, "to meet thy corpse, for death is near thee." And he said:

Why have you come from the church?

O sons of sweet sounding words.

Do not conceal from me, by our God in heaven

Tell me the truth.

Clerics:

We have come to meet your body,

So that the stories can be told.

We will take you to Tuilén,

Oh good man without conscience.

Mac Erca:

My body should be beautifully cleaned.

Masan and Casan, in the morning,

Take my mutilated body to Cairnech.

Clerics

We will carry your pitiable body

Until it reaches Tuilén.

It will be a major cause of sadness

In the noble land of Ireland.

Mac Erca:

Oh Clerics, I feel great pain,

As though my soul separates from my body.

Were it not for your guidance

 I would be cold in a strange land.

Clerics:

By Cairnech and Tigernach the vigorous,

And the high and noble Saints of Ireland,

We would not let you be in cold hell,
O brave hero with the mighty sword.

Mac Erca:
I ask forgiveness from the king of heaven,
With all my heart.
My pure body is under your protection tonight,
Because you have come to me.

27. The clerics marked out a church there in the Brug, and told
him to dig its trench in honour of the great Lord of the Elements.
"It shall be done," said he. Then he began digging the trench, so
that it was then for the first time that the green of the Brug was
injured. And he was telling the clerics his own tidings, and
making God a fervent repentance. He said:

My wrath has ended here,
Since I came over sea to Erin.
I remember the number of years,
I have never seen a day, lasting the fame,
Without a hero's head and a triumph over him.
I was eleven years without finding domain.
Until then, there was no night
without a head of Leinster or Munster.
I was myself twenty years
In the kingdom of Eogan, son of Niall;

I had every night without a doubt

A head Of Ulster and Connaught.

I was twenty-five years without fail

In the kingship of Ireland.

There was no night so far

Without the slaying of someone in Ireland.

Two years I was east in Alba,

I have killed my grandsire,

I have brought a host there into troubles,

By my deeds Loarn fell.

Two years I was afterwards

In kingship over Danes,

There has been no night there at

Without the heads of two on stakes.

Here is my true confession,

In the presence of the king of kings.

I have been much of my days without weakness,

And I have not been near death.

Now after this confession the clerics blessed water for him, and be partook of the Body of Christ, and made to God a fervent repentance. And he told them to relate to Cairnech how he had made his confession and repentance. So then he said:

Faithful faithful is my wretched body of clay,

Remember, remember my beloved form.

Fearful, fearful is the everlasting beast,
Cold, cold is the stone against my side.

Fearful fearful is the coldness of hell,
The ever-narrow place forever through the ages.
My desire for this place was always distant,
To be [lying] east-west in the graveyards of the Kings.

My body in the mound, my body through the ages,
My body, truly, my body fearful of fire,
Wine, wine in place of water, no lie,
My dead body, it goes and is found by Eve.

'Til Doomsday, 'til Doomsday no tribute now,
A meeting, a meeting of my men in assembly.
My power, my power comes to an end in bondage,
Ever true, true this is my grudging arrival.

My burial, burial as a mighty king,
Truly, truly my victory has preceded me.
Evil that it happened to me in my house,
My body, faithful, faithful.

29. The clerics remained for that night in the church of the Brug, and the king went to Cletech and sat there at his lady's right hand. Sin asked him what bad interrupted his combat on that day.

"The clerics came to me," he answered, "and they put the sign of the Cross of Christ over my face, and then I saw nothing save fern and stone and puff-balls. And since there was no one there to fight me, I came away." Then Sin spoke:

Never believe the clerics,
For they chant nothing save unreason.
Follow not their unmelodious verses,
For they do not revere righteousness.
Cleave not to the clerics of churches,
If you desire life without treachery:
Better Sin, I as a friend here,
Let not repentance come to thee.

Muircertach.
I will be always along with you,
O fair damsel without evil plight;
Likelier to me is your countenance
Than the churches of the clerics.

31. Then Sin beguiled his mind and came between him and the teachings of the clerics, and on that night she made a magical wine for the king and his troops. The seventh night she was at her magic, on the eve of Wednesday after Samhain (Halloween) precisely. When the hosts were intoxicated there came the sigh of

a great wind. "This is 'the sigh of a winter-night,'" said the king. And Sin said:

I am Rough-Wind,
A daughter of fair nobles:
Winter-night is my name,
I am everywhere at the same time.

Sigh and Wind
Winter-Night so,
I speak the truth,
That your end is coming soon.

If you come thither,
To the door of your house,
Death will come to your lips.
In these words, you will find knowledge.

32. And then she caused a great snowstorm there; and never had come a noise of battle that was greater than the shower of thick snow that poured there at that time, and from the northwest, precisely it came. Then the king came forth and went into the house again, and began reproaching the storm; and he said:

Evil is the night tonight,
Never came one as bad,

I will never see such a night again.

Sin:

The energy of Cletech is cold,

Your age has been shortened.

Do not say my timeless names,

An evil fate threatens if you do.

Mac Erca.

I will not state them and

I will also avoid them all,

This I declare tonight,

I have no doubt that misfortune is evil.

33. When the feasting ended, then the hosts lay down, and in no one of them was the strength of a woman in childbed. Then the king lay down on his couch, and a heavy sleep fell upon him. Then he made a great screaming out of his slumber and awoke from his sleep. "What is that?" said the damsel. "A great host of demons has appeared to me," he answered; whereupon he said:

A form of red fire has appeared to me,

And many noble spirits,

The pitiful decline of a great army,

Destroyed by the treachery of magic,

The house of Cletech as a fatal fire,

Round my head blazing forever,
The Clan of Niall in wrongful suffering
Through the spells of witches,
Their shields are wearily laid down
By arrangement of the curse.
Weapons that are crossed,
Wounds that come quickly,
The cry of a mighty host under red fire,
This is what has appeared to me.

34. The king rose up, for the vision which he beheld did not let him sleep, and he came forth out of the house, and in the little church of the Brug he saw a little fire by the clerics. He came to them and said, "There is neither strength nor vigor in me tonight." And he related his vision and his dream. "And it is hard," said he, "to show prowess tonight even though hosts of foreign enemies should attack me, because of the weakness in which we are and the badness of the night." So then the clerics began instructing him. He came in at once and there he said:

Full evil is this storm (sin) tonight
To the clerics in their camp;
They dare not ever sleep,
Due to the roughness of the night's storms.

Sin

Why do you say my name, O man,

O son of Erc and Muiredach?

You will find death—feast without disgrace—

Sleep not in the House of Cletech.

Muircertach.

Tell me, you griefless lady,

What number of the hosts shall fall by me?

Hide it not from me, tell without commandment,

What number will fall by my right hand?

Sin

No one will fall by you to the floor,

O son of Erc of the high rank:

You, O king, have surely ended:

Your Strength has come to nothing.

Muircertach.

A great defect is my being without strength,

O noble Sin of many forms,

Often have I killed a fierce warrior,

Though tonight I am under oppression.

Sin

Many have fallen by your effort,

O son of Loarn's daughter!

You have brought a multitude of hosts to silence;

Alas, that you are in evil easel.

35. "That is true, O damsel," said he; "death is near to me; for it was foretold that my death and the death of Loarn my grandfather would be alike; for he did not fall in battle, but was burnt alive. "Sleep then tonight," said the damsel, "and leave to me to watch you and to guard you from the hosts; and, if it is your fate, the house will not be burnt over you tonight." "Truly, there is coming, with designs upon us, Tuathal Maelgarb son of Cormac Caich son of Cairbre son of Niall of the Nine Hostages."
"Though Tuathal with all his hosts be coming with designs upon you, have you no fear of him tonight," said the damsel, "and sleep now."

36. Then he went into his bed and asked the damsel for a drink, and she cast a sleeping charm upon that deceptive wine, so that when he drank a draught of it, it made him drunk and feeble, without sap or strength. Then he slept heavily and he saw a vision, to wit, that he went in a ship to sea, and his ship foundered, and a taloned griffin came to him and carried him into her nest, and then he and the nest were burnt, and the griffin fell with him.

37. The king awoke and ordered his vision to be taken to his foster-brother Dub Da Rinn[218] son of the druid Saignen[219], and

Dub Da Rinn gave him the meaning of it as so: "This is the ship wherein you have been, as such, the ship of your princedom on the sea of life, and with you steering it. This is the ship that foundered, and your life is to come to an end. This is the taloned griffin that has carried you into her nest, the woman that is in your company, to make you intoxicated, and to bring you with her into her bed, and to detain you in the house of Cletech so that it will burn over you. Now the griffin that fell with you is the woman who will die as well because of you. This then is the significance of that vision."

38. The king then slept heavily after Sin had cast the sleep-charm upon him. Now while he was in that sleep Sin arose and arranged the spears and the javelins of the hosts in readiness in the doors and then turned all their points toward the house. She formed by magic many crowds and multitudes throughout the house and the sidewalk, and then she entered the bed.

39. It was then that the king awoke from his sleep. "What is it?" asked the damsel.
"A host of demons has appeared to me, burning the house upon me and slaughtering my people at the door." "You cannot be hurt by that," said the damsel; "it only seemed so."

---

[218] Dub Da Rinn – The dark spear??. Mac Erca's foster brother a druid. Compare Arthurs spear Rhonn.

[219] Meaning Saignen (lightning) was Mac Erca's foster father, a druid who raised him. Saignen –lightning, compare Arthurs sword Caledfwlch –lightning sword.

40. Now when they were thus in converse, they heard the crash of the burning house, and the shout of the host of demons and wizardry around it. "Who is around the house?" asked the king. Said Sin, "Tuathal Maelgarb son of Cormac Caib son of Niall of the Nine Hostages, with his armies. He is here taking vengeance on you for the battle of Grainne." And the king knew not that this was untrue, and that no human host was surrounding the house.

41. He arose swiftly and came to seek his arms, and found no one to answer him. The damsel went forth from the house, and he followed her at once, and he met a host in front of him, so that he went heavily through them. From the door he returned to his bed. The hosts thereupon went forth, and no one of them escaped without wounding or burning.

42. Then the king came again towards the door, and between him and it were the embers and hails of fire. When the fire had filled the doorway[220] and the entire house around, he found no shelter for himself, so he got into a cask of wine, and therein he was drowned, as he went under it every second time for fear of the fire. Then the fire fell on his head, and five feet of his length was burnt; but the wine kept the rest of his body from burning.

---

[220] The piercing by spears placed by Sin in the doorway as well has been left out of this version, so disguising the three fold death of the earlier versions.

43. The day after, when the morning came, the clerics Masan and Casan and Cridan came to the king and carried his body to the Boyne and washed it.

44. Cairnech also came to him and made great grief in bewailing him, and said, "A great loss to Ireland today is Mac Erca, one of the four best men that have gained possession of Erin without trickery and without force, namely, Muircertach mac Erca, Niall of the Nine Hostages, Conn the Hundred-Fighter, and Ugaine Mor."

The Life of Mac Erca known to me.
No small number of years have I watched him
Since that first night he was born,
Until afterwards, he became as nothing.

Ten years for him in the house of the Druid
Saignen, of a multitude of cattle.
The storm (hero) of great endurance,
Muircertach, strong and powerful.

Two years for him at the house of king
Muiredach the great, of good worth,
Until afterwards, with sorrow he parted,
Afflicting Muiredach with much grief.

Two specific years for him to be

In the house of Loarn, the valorous Erc,

Was Muircertach without avarice,

Until he committed the murder of a relative.

He was thirty years

Amongst the Britons, no lie

In that time taking possession

Of the Saxon and Briton hosts.

Ten years after that

They assembled in a severe attack;

The Saxons and the Britons, without grief,

Their assembly aimed towards Ireland

Twenty years of much strength

As King of Northern Ireland,

In his father's estate since birth

Muiredach the great, son of Eoghan.

The king of all Ireland [Mac Erca],

The descendent of Eoghan in High kingship.

Twenty five years without end,

Until his life was cut short.

45. And the body was lifted up by Cairnech, to be carried to Tuilen and there interred.

46. Then Duinsech, the wife of Muircertach, met the clerics while the corpse was among them, and she made a great, mournful lamentation, struck her palms together, and leaned her back against the ancient tree in Anach Reil; and a burst of gore broke from her heart in her breast, and straightway she died of grief for her husband. Then the clerics put the queen's corpse along with the corpse of the king. And then said Cairnech:

Duinsech, Mac Erca's noble wife,
Let her grave be dug by you here,
The daughter of the king of Connaght clann.
She gave birth to Fergus and Domnall.

Let Duinsech be placed in the tomb,
Such a pity to suffer death.
Daughter of Dauch, we dug her mound,
Until she is buried in her grave.

Twenty-five years of solid time,
In the high kingship of Ireland,
Until the king was caused to depart from us
Mother of his children, Duinsech.

47. Then the queen was buried and her grave was made. The king was buried near the church on the north side, and Cairnech declared the king's character and uttered this lay:

The grave of the King of Ailech will abide forever
In Tuilen, everyone will hear of it
On the Road of Asail it will be long lasting
Here in this twisting place of famous hosts.

Good was every place during the time of
Muirchertach grandson of Eoghan the fair.
He did not come to Ireland with treachery,
The highest king over him gave him victory

Thirty feet of height in truth,
Was Muircertach, supreme king of Ailech.
No one who came afterwards,
Was equal in strength or reach.

Twenty-five feet in truth
Of the kings body has arrived here,
Five feet having been burnt.
The wine in the vat was not deep enough.

No one will ever force a hostage from
The race of the Kings of Ailech,

Who are feared by every strong house
That is known throughout Ireland.

In the places of the great Irish clerics of old,
The sins of Mac Erca led to his fate.
It will be a long day before I forget this place
All of my life I will watch his grave.

48. When the clerics had finished the burial they saw coming toward them a solitary woman, beautiful and shining, robed in a green mantle with its fringe of golden thread. A smock of priceless silk was about her. She reached the place where the clerics were and saluted them, and so the clerics saluted her. And they perceived upon her an appearance of sadness and sorrow and they recognized that she it was that had ruined the king. Cairnech asked tidings of her and said:

Tell us your origin,
O damsel, without darkening;
You have wrought our shame,
Though beauteous is thy body:
You have killed the King of Tara,
With many of his households,
By an awful, evil deed.

Sin:

I can tell you,

I can make no denial,

Oh Clerics of power and knowledge,

In exchange for my body,

Give the sky my soul,

I will tell you then,

What I took with fierceness,

From the hero of the world.

Cairnech:

If you do oh maiden,

Sorrowful shall be your confession,

Your penance shall be keen,

The irony is a great testimony,

Forgiveness to each man,

We bring to all things,

Through the supreme King of all,

God himself in this place.

49. Then the clerics asked her who she herself was, or who was her father or her mother, and what cause she had from the king that she should ruin him.

"Sin" she replied, "is my name, and Sige son of Dian son of Tren is my father. Muircertach mac Erca killed my father, my mother, and my sister in the Battle of Cerb on the Boyne, and also destroyed in that battle all the Old-Tribes of Tara and my fatherland." So then Cairnech said and Sin replied:

Cairnech.

Say, oh Sin, a statement without question,

Tell truly who was you father,

And what prompted you, oh woman

And who is your family.

Sin.

I am the daughter of Sige the slender

Of the tribe of Tara above the Boyne

I will not hide the truth

I will put it in order.

Muircertach killed my father,

He has shared great booty in combat,

At the ford of far Cerba,

Called the ford of Sige.

Sige had mastered trickery,

With his speech he brought a host into trouble,

There was no one equal in battle,

No river in Banba so cloaked in red [blood].

Cairnech:

Dearer to you is the father that loved you

Than to Muircertach descendant of Niall.

By no means feel forsaken ,

Oh gentle smooth and melodious maiden.

Sin:

Myself, I will die of grief for him,

The high-king of the western world,

And for the guilt of the sore tribulations

That I brought on the sovereign of Erin.

I made poison for him, alas!

Which overpowered the king of the noble hosts,

Who before had existed in this place,

Grief I have for him who has departed.

For three months I danced with him

Until he fell to my disdain,

After him I will not exist.

Good fortune to you oh great Abbott.

50. Then she confessed to Cairnech, and to God she made fervent repentance, as was taught her, and she went in obedience to Cairnech, and straightway died of grief for the king. So Cairnech said that a grave should be made for her, and that she should be

put under the award of the earth. It was done as the cleric ordered, and he said

Sin, not dear were her doings,
Until this day in which we are,
Cold misfortune has brought justice,
Her mocking speech has brought lasting trouble.

They will bury her body underground,
When it has been washed without delay.
It is no longer her body but a corpse that comes.
No submission for the daughter of Sige.

Sige was not a man without valour,
He was not slow to the plunder,
He gave the satisfaction of wealth to Tara.
Sharp was the vengeance of Sin for her relatives.

Of Sin (Sheen)

Many shall be her names who will put one astray.
Unloving is the woman whose name is Sheen,
For whose sake fire shall burn the king,
In the house of Cletty, wine shall drown him.

She was the wanton woman, who slew the heir of Niall,

Her name is in every place and road on a winter's day,

The sigh of a rapid storm without reproach

And the groan of the milking cow.

Without doubt, these are where you will hear her name.

51. As for Cairnech, he showed great care for Muircertach's soul, but he did not bring it out of hell. Howbeit he composed a prayer, which from its beginning was called Parce mihi Domine ("Spare me, O Lord"), etc., and he repeated it continually for the sake of the soul of the king. Whereupon an angel came to Cairnech and told him that whoever would sing that prayer continually would without doubt be a dweller in Heaven. So then said the angel:

Whoever should sing strongly,

The prayer of Cairnech of the mysteries,

'Twould be enough to succor

Judas, who was the worst ever born.

You have (died and) gone to the sky Mac Erca ,

Above us now for our fervent prayer,

You have gone, forever on high,

With your bright body that belongs in hell.

Cairnech:

I give thanks to Christ who loves me,

And the holy angel who watches over me,

It has been pleasant in my time,

To be in the presence of the good angel.

There are twenty five years exactly,

Since I arrived here from Rome,

Until this very night.

52. So far the Death of Muircertach Mac Erca, as Cairnech related it, and Tigernach and Ciaran and Mochta and Tuathal Maelgarb; and it was written and revised by those holy clerics, commemorating it for everyone from that time to this.

Conclusions

The story of Mac Erca is a fascinating tale of heroic adventure mixed with pseudo-history and finished off with a mythical three fold death. As can be appreciated now, the stories in the *Lebor Bretnach* and *Yellow Book of Lecan* are pre Galfridian in their dating, meaning they existed before Geoffrey of Monmouth had written his great work on Arthur in the mid twelfth century. They may even have existed in the ninth century, the time when the first tales of Arthur were being written down in Wales. Whether these tales developed side by side, independently or fed off each other over the centuries is a matter for a larger work of study. This present study merely introduces this character of Irish history to Arthuriana and to a wider public audience.

What is evident is that the story of Mac Erca mirrors that of Arthur's. He exists in the same timeframe, he defeats the same peoples, he has powerful weapons and his wife's name mirrors that of Arthurs when translated into Welsh. His own name can be interpreted as an Arthur name. It is fairly certain then, that Mac Erca is the warrior the Irish considered their Arthur.

The fact of the matter though is that the Irish took their story to a more believable level than did Geoffrey. Mac Erca not only defeats a real life Clovis as opposed to Geoffrey's unknown Lucius, but he is also made to marry the daughter of Clovis who gives birth to Constantine, the progenitor of the British kings. His other son, from his first wife carries the name of Badon itself, the greatest victory of the Britons over the Saxons. Is this a coincidence or do we really have the first evidence of someone named after the great battle?

Whether Mac Erca was really the same person as Muircertach Mac Muiredaig is a question that will take further study as would be the question as to who Mac Erca really was if he wasn't identical to Muircertach. The name *Muircertach* itself appears to be a late form and may not have existed anyway in the fifth and sixth centuries. There is also the question as to whether Mac Erca was an Irishman possibly of the clan of Conall, adopted by the O'Neills or whether he was a Briton adopted into Irish genealogies much like St Ninian was by two separate Irish families and genealogies by the late seventh century.

We know Mac Erca was historical, having been mentioned by Adamnan in the late seventh century and by his mention in the *Bail Chuin* of the early to mid seventh century, as well as the Annal entries that show the older spelling of Erce.

Was Mac Erca the man known to the Welsh and Britons as Arthur? I have made tentative links with the name and its incarnations over the years, from its Ogham and early Latin forms to the links with the Irish words for sky and heaven and for the subsequent suggestion of a possible meaning of `son of Ursus' in effect `son of the bear'. As Arthur means *bear* in Welsh and I have shown that *Erc* could evolve into *Erth*, also meaning *bear* in Welsh, then the possibility that Mac Erca could have been an *Arthur* is certainly a possibility.

In a larger work I will endeavor to answer some of the problems mentioned above and come to conclusions concerning Arthur, King of the Britons, but for now I hope you have enjoyed the tales of the Irish Arthur, who accomplished everything that the Welsh Arthur is said to have done and in exactly the same time frame.

Appendix

Appendix consisting of the original tales from the Irish HB and the *Baile Chuind Chétchathaig*:

Of The Miracles of Cairnech Here.

SARRAN assumed the sovereignty of Britain after this, and established his power over the Saxons and Cruithnians. And he took to wife the daughter of the king of Alban, viz., Babona, daughter of Loarn, son of Erc. And it was not she that was married to him, but her sister, viz., Erc, daughter of Loarn, until she eloped with Muiredhach, son of Eoghan, son of Niall, to Eri, and she bore him four sons, viz. Muircheartach Mac Erca, and Fearadhach, and Tighearnach, and Maian. And Sarran had issue by Babona; and there were begotten by them five sons, viz., Luirig, and Cairnech, and Bishop Dallain, and Caemlach; and he *i.e.* Sarran died after victory and after triumph in the house of Martin.

Luirig then succeeded *to the throne*, and he extended his power over the Saxons, and he forcibly built a fort within the precincts of the monastery of Cairnech his brother. Muircheartach Mac Erca happened to be at that time with the king of Britain, learning military science, after he was expelled from Ireland for having killed the Crossans, and after having been subsequently expelled from Alba, for having killed his grandfather, Loarn, king of Alba.

It happened that he was at that time getting his arms consecrated by Cairnech, the son of his mother's sister; then Cairnech said to him, 'Thou shalt be king of Eri and of Britain for ever, and shalt go to heaven after, provided thou canst but prevent Luirig from exercising his power against the Church.' Then Mac Erca went to the king, and after he came he told his message, viz.: 'Build not thy city' (*said he*) 'in the precincts of Cairnech the bishop.' 'As God is my judge,' says Luirig, 'I think more of the power of the pet wild fawn he has, than of his own *power*, or *of the power* of the Lord God whom he adores.' Mac Erca returned to Cairnech, and told him the result. Great wrath suddenly seized Cairnech, et dixit, 'My prayer to my Lord, to my God, is, that that very fawn may be the cause of his death, and by thy *hand*, O Mac Erca!' Cairnech then commanded Mac Erca to go forth and destroy his brother, and he *Mac Erca* immediately took upon himself to fight him; and he went forth at the command of Cairnech to destroy the king. And God worked a great miracle there for Cairnech, viz. he sent a wild fawn out of the mountain into the king's assembly, and the host all went in pursuit of it except the king himself and his women. Et dixit Mac Erca, 'If you had been just, my Lord, towards your cleric, it is certain that it would give increased happiness to have the royal robe on Luirig.' Then Mac Erca thrust his battle staff into the king's side, so that it was balanced: and he returned to his cleric, and the head *of the king* with him, as a token; et dixit, 'Lo, here is thy brother's head for thee, O Cairnech.' Et dixit Cairnech, 'Leave me the bone, and eat thou the marrow, and every third coarb shall be thine for ever, here and in Eri.'

Then he (Mac Erca) took the hostages and the power of the district *into his own hands, conjointly* with Cairnech, for seven years, as also the supreme sovereignty of Britain, and Cat, and Orc, and Saxonland.

And Mac Erca *then* committed an additional sin, that is, he took to himself the wife of Luirig, after many battles and conflicts with the king of France, to take his daughter from him, until at last the daughter fell into Mac Erca's hands, and she bare him four sons, viz. Constantine, and Gaedhal-Ficht (from whom descend the kings of Britain, and the kings of Britain-Cornn); Nellenn (a quo gens Nellan), and Scannal, the other son, a quo gens Scannail; i. e. it is in Eri the descendants of the two last are.

Now a great synod of the clergy of Europe was made at Tours of Martin, viz., three hundred and thirty-seven bishops, with the coarb of Peter, to meet Cairnech, Bishop of Tours and Britain-Cornn, and of all the British, to cast out every heresy, and to reduce every country to the discipline of the Church. And the chieftainship of the martyrs of the world was given to Cairnech, because martyrdom was his own choice. And Cairnech found thrice fifty bishops who made it also their choice to accompany Cairnech in pilgrimage, and that number went to Lien in pilgrimage for the sake of Mac Erca and Muiredhach.

Cairnech then set out to the Britons of Cornn or Carnticeon, and a city was built by him under ground, in order that he might not see the earth, nor the country, nor the sky; and he increased the strength and sovereignty of Mac Erca for a year, and he (i.e. *Cairnech*) came to Eri before him, so that he was the first bishop of the Clann-Niall and of Temhar (*Tara*), and he was the first martyr and the first monk of Eri, and the first Brehon of the men of Eri also.

Now, after this the Franks and the Saxons made war against Mac Erca, and he destroyed their country and their cities after a long contest; and the country and the power of the territories adjacent to him were also destroyed by the greatness of his power and of his strength; and after this he came with a large fleet to take the sovereignty of Eri. He landed at Fan-na-long on the Boyne, where he burned his ships, from which *circumstance* comes *the name of* Fan-na-long; and he killed the provincial *kings* of Ireland afterwards, and took their sovereignty by right for ever, for himself and for his descendants. And then the power and strength of Britain was destroyed after him.

The Ecstasy of Conn of the Hundred Battles[221]

RIA MS 23 N 10

Art shall drink it after forty nights, a mighty hero, until he shall die at Mucruime. Mac Con of the race of Lugaid Loígde, who shall play for a day and a week against Fergus Dubdétach, until they shall die at Bri, through seeking a battle which he shall deliver towards Crinnae. Corbmac shall drink it up; an ancient drink; a pleasant warrior; he shall die at Scoilicc; he shall be a glorious man over her; he shall wash her. Coirpre shall drink it, a fitting contestant with righteousness of rule. Firachri shall demand it; the great deceits of Meath shall advance to the distant sea, till Broadfaced Dáire shall distribute it for a plenteous month. Fécho, unwitting man of fire, from whom they shall be assessed in regard to tax, shall demand it. Muiredach Tírech shall be thirty-yeared. Glorious Crimthann shall bind her with a bond, broad fierce shape beneath foot, till Níall shall be extolled; (...) battles of boundaries, till fierce Loígaire shall be grieved by the coming of the Adzeheads, crossbeams of houses, bent trees, they used to carry blossoms, a rampart, a fort. An excellent champion, Coirpre, shall drink it. **Feirce Lugaid of noble great drinking shall be approached: ordeal of battle. A glorious man upon him, Mac Ercéne.** Óengarb shall take it with fame of fierce spear. Aíd, glorious champion, shall take it, Aíd Olláin who shall

---

221 Murphey, G. "Two Sources in Thurneysen's Heldensage". Ériu 15 (1952) 144-56. Thurneysen, R. (ed), 'Baile Chuind Chétchathaig nach der Handschrift von Druim Snechta', Zu irischen Handschriften und Litteraturdenkmälern (Berlin 1912) 48-52.

smite a smiting. Diarmait's justice shall be on her: Diarmati, by whom forts shall be ruled with glorious (...), shall demand it, till towards Irthine (?) (...) Féachno (...) over her. Noble Suibne shall be better. Domnall shall be a glorious Óengus. Bláthmac shall approach it, [and] Diarmait, the other's grandson. He who shall celebrate the celebration, rule of exemptions, rule of guilts, rule of slayers, is the two-hundred-yeared Éilimm who was: Snechta Fína [, i.e. Fínṡnechta aliter Fínnachta] who shall pour shall drink it: rule from Níall to Níall; the descendant of Níall is everyone's Níall: hostages are pledged; fire approchaes thee; through him bracken shall be red and rough; perhaps in the third month over a year he shall die by the sea: great the gloom and loss to the world's generations. A sixty-year king, after hosts it is his; he shall die by blood; fierce battle shall injure them, loss, death. Flann of Assal shall be over her, a glorious heir: he shall powerfully bind her with a handful of hostages. Furbaide shall approach it, better thane very man over her, a king good in regard to judgement, good in regard to splendour, glorious ruler upon whom shall be a heavy (...) smiting as a result for which there shall be death at Brī. The rule of Cailech, strongly shall it be known over her. Glúnṡalach shall be over her; a race who sides are very red, he shall bind them with hostages; he shall seize Ross; he shall rule Munster, good battle, first (...) of Irthine (?), glorious ruler over Tara. A kin-slaying man, prone to unjust judgements, shall approach it; he shall drink it to the pit of the world; encircling Saxons, he shall drive them from Corc; he is the king of Munster of great lordships in Tara.

Finit.

Bibliography and cited works

Abrams, Lesley and Carley, James P. eds. *The Archaeology and History of Glastonbury Abbey: Essays in Honour of the Ninetieth Birthday* C.A. Ralegh Radford. Woodbridge, Suffolk: Boydell & Brewer, 1991.

Anderson, Graham. *King Arthur in Antiquity*. New York: Routledge, 2003.

Ashe, Geoffrey. *A Certain Very Ancient Book: Traces of an Arthurian Source in Geoffrey of Monmouth's History*, Speculum. 1981.

Baring-Gould,S. – Fisher, John. *The Lives of The British Saints: The Saints of Wales, Cornwall and Irish Saints Vol 2*, Honourable Society of Cymmrodorion, Kessinger Publishing, 2005

Barnwell, P. S. *Emperor, Prefects & Kings: The Roman West, 395-565*. Chapel Hill, NC: University of North Carolina Press, 1992.

Barron, W. R. J., ed. *The Arthur of the English: The Arthurian Legend in Medieval English Life and Literature*. Cardiff, Wales: University of Wales Press, 1999.

Bieler, Ludwig. *Ireland: Harbinger of the Middle Ages*. 1st ed. London: Oxford University Press, 1963.

Blair, Peter Hunter. *Roman Britain and Early England, 55 B.C.-A.D. 871*. Edinburgh: Thomas Nelson & Sons, 1963.

Brook, G. L. *An Introduction to Old English*. Manchester, England: Manchester University Press, 1955.

Bury, J. B. *The Life of St. Patrick and His Place in History*. London: Macmillan, 1905.

Byrne, Francis J. *Irish Kings and High Kings*. Four Courts Press 2001.

Calise, J. M. P. *Pictish Sourcebook : Documents of Medieval Legend and Dark Age History*. Westport, CT: Greenwood Press, 2002.

Carney, James. *Studies in Irish Literature and History*. Dublin: Dublin Institute for Advanced Studies, 1955.

Chambers, E. K. *Arthur of Britain*. London: Sidgwick & Jackson, 1927.

Charles-Edwards, T. M. *Early Christian Ireland*. Cambridge, England: Cambridge University Press, 2000.

The Chronicle of Ireland. Trans. Vol. 1. Liverpool, England: University of Liverpool Press, 2006.

The Social Background to Irish Perigrinatio. In Celtica 11 (1976) pp. 43–59.

Collingwood, R. G., and J. N. L. Myres. *Roman Britain and the English Settlements*. New York: Biblo and Tannen, 1990.

Connolly, S. J., ed. *The Oxford Companion to Irish History*. Oxford: Oxford University Press, 1999.

Delivre, Fabrice. *The Foundations of Primatial Claims in the Western Church (Eleventh–Thirteenth Centuries)*. The Journal of Ecclesiastical History, 2008

Dillon, Myles. *Translated, ed. Ceart Ui Neill*, Studia Celtica. Volume. University of Wales Board of Celtic Studies, University of Wales Press., 1966

Dobbs, C. – Maighreád. *"The Ban-shenchus"*. Revue Celtique. vol. 47-49

Dooley, Ann. *Tales of the Elders of Ireland*. (Acallam na Senórach) Oxford University Press, 1999.

Donnchadha, Lil Nic. *Aided Muircertach Meic Erca* . Dublin Institute for advanced studies 1980.

Downham, Clare. *Viking Kings Of Britain and Ireland - the dynasty of Ívarr to A.D. 1014*. Dunedin Academic Press 2007

Duignan, Leonie. *The Echtrae as an Early Irish Literary Genre*. School of Celtic Studies 2010.

Dumville, David. *Histories and Pseudo-Histories of the Insular Middle Ages*. Variorum, Gower Publishing Group, 1990.

St Patrick A.D. 493-1993. Boydell Press 1993.

Celtic Essays, 2001-2007. University of Aberdeen, 2007.

Chronicles and Annals of Medieval Ireland & Wales. The Boydell Press, 1984.

Ireland and Britain in Tain Bo Fraich, In ÉtC 32 pp. 175–187, 1996.

Ellis, Peter Berresford. *Eyewitness to Irish History*. Hoboken, NJ: Wiley, 2004.

Everard, J. A. *Brittany and the Angevins: Province and Empire, 1158-1203*. Cambridge, England: Cambridge University Press, 2000.

Fanning, S. *"Clovis Augustus and Merovingian Imitatio Imperii."* *The World of Gregory of Tours*. Boston: Brill, 2002. null44-null45.

Geddes, Michael. *Miscellaneous Tracts. Vol.II.* circa 1714

Gidlow, Christopher. *The Reign of Arthur from History to Legend*. Sutton Publishing Ltd. Gloucester, 2004.

Gillies, H. Cameron. *The Place names of Argyle*. David Nutt; First Edition, 1906

Gillingham, John, ed. *Anglo-Norman Studies XXIII: Proceedings of the Battle Conference, 2000*. Woodbridge, England: Boydell Press, 2001.

Glancy, Jennifer A. *Slavery in Early Christianity*. New York: Oxford University Press, 2002.

Gransden, Antonia. *Historical Writing in England*. London: Routledge, 1996.

Grant, Michael. *Greek and Roman Historians: Information and Misinformation*. New York: Routledge, 1995.

Green, Tom. *Concepts of Arthur*. Tempus Publishing, 2007

Guyonvarc'h, J. *Le Mort De Muirchertach, Fils De Erc.* Annales. Économies, Sociétés, Civilisations, Année 1983, Volume 38, Numéro 5

GuÉrard, Albert. *France: A Modern History.* Ann Arbor, MI: University of Michigan Press, 1959.

Hanning, Robert W. *The Vision of History in Early Britain: from Gildas to Geoffrey of Monmouth.* New York: Columbia University Press, 1966.

Harbus, Antonina. *Helena of Britain in Medieval Legend.* Rochester, NY: D.S. Brewer, 2002.

Harper-Bill, Christopher, and Elisabeth Van Houts, eds. *A Companion to the Anglo-Norman World.* Suffolk, England: Boydell Press, 2003.

Harries, Jill. *Sidonius Apollinaris and the Fall of Rome, AD 407-485.* Oxford: Clarendon Press, 1994.

Higham, N. J. *King Arthur: Myth-Making and History.* London, Routledge, 2002.

Hodgkin, Thomas. *The Barbarian Invasions Of The Roman Empire Vol.1. The Visigothic Invasion.* Clarendon Press, 1880. Reprinted by The Folio Society, London, 2000.

Hubert, Henri. *The Rise of the Celts.* New York: Biblo and Tannen, 1966.

Hudson, Benjamin T. *Kings of Celtic Scotland.* Westport, CT: Greenwood Press, 1994.

Prophecy of Berchan – Irish and Scottish High Kings In the Early Middle Ages., Praeger Publishers, 1996.

Hughes, A. J. *The Virgin St. Duinsech and Her Three Ulster Churches near Strangford Lough, County Down.* Centre for Irish and Celtic Studies, University of Ulster at Coleraine, Celtica 23, 1999

Idat., and Prosp. "*Chapter III Relations of Romans with the Invaders.*" Roman Society in the Last Century of the Western Empire. 2nd Rev. ed. London: Macmillan, 1921. 346-382.

Ireland, Colin. *Aldfrith of Northumbria and the Irish Genealogies. Celtica* 22, 1990

Jackson, Kenneth Hurlstone. *A Celtic Miscellany: Translations from the Celtic Literatures*. Cambridge, MA: Harvard University Press, 1951.

Jackson, W. H., and S. A. Ranawake, eds. *The Arthur of the Germans: The Arthurian Legend in Medieval German and Dutch Literature*. Cardiff, Wales: University of Wales Press, 2000.

James E. - Luscombe David E. - McKitterick, Rosamond. – Reuter, Timothy. *The new Cambridge medieval history. –* Cambridge University Press – 2006

Jones, Gwyn. – Jones, Thomas. *The Mabinogian*. Dragons Dream B.V. 1982

Jones, Mari C. *Language Obsolescence and Revitalization: Linguistic Change in Two Sociolinguistically Contrasting Welsh Communities*. Oxford: Clarendon Press, 1998.

Jones, Michael E. *The End of Roman Britain*. Ithaca, NY: Cornell University Press, 1996.

Keating, G. *History of Ireland*. Circa 1662.

Kirby, D. P. *The Earliest English Kings*. London: Routledge, 2000.

Knapp, James A. *Illustrating the Past in Early Modern England: The Representation of History in Printed Books*. Ashgate Publishing; illustrated edition, 2003.

Lacy, Norris J. *The New Arthurian Encyclopedia*. Garland, 1991

Lacey, Brian. *Cenél Conail and the Donegal Kingdoms 500-800*. Four Courts Press 2006

Lionarons, Joyce Tally. *The Medieval Dragon: The Nature of the Beast in Germanic Literature*. Enfield Lock, England: Hisarlik, 1998.

Littleton, C. Scott, Malcor, Linda, *From Scythia to Camelot: A Radical Reassessment of the Legends of King Arthur,* *the Knights of the Round Table and the Holy Grail.* New York, Garland, 2000.

Lloyd-Morgan, C. Arthurian *Literature XXI: Celtic Arthurian* Material: Celtic Arthurian Material v. 21 2004.

Loomis, Roger Sherman. *The Development of Arthurian Romance*. London: Hutchinson University Library, 1963.

Scotland and the Arthurian Legend. Columbia University. Proceedings of the Society 1955/56.

Medieval English Verse and Prose. New York 1948

Luscombe, James E., McKitterick, David E., Rosamond, Reuter, Timothy. *The new Cambridge medieval history*. Cambridge University Press – 2006.

Lydon, James. The *Making of Ireland: From Ancient Times to the Present*. London: Routledge, 1998.

MacNeil, John (Eion). *History and Grammar of Ogham Inscriptions*. Proceedings of the Royal Irish Academy, House of Dubros 1909.

Poems by Flann Mainistrech on the Dynasties of Ailech, Mide and Brega. Archivium Hibernicum, Vol. 2 1913.

Phases of Irish History. Dublin 1920.

Macquarrie, Alan. *"1 The Kings of Strathclyde, C.400- 1018."* *Medieval Scotland: Crown, Lordship and Community*: Essays Presented to G.W.S Barrow. Ed. Alexander Grant andKeith J. Stringer. Edinburgh: Edinburgh University Press, 1998. 1-19.

MacLysaght, Edward. *The Surnames of Ireland*. Irish Academic Press, 1989.

Mainistrech, Flann, - MacNeil, John. *Poems by Flann Mainistrech on the Dynasties of Ailech, Mide and Brega* Archivium Hibernicum, Vol. 2 1913

Malcor, Linda and Littleton, C. Scott. *From Scythia to Camelot: A Radical Reassessment of the Legends of King Arthur, the Knights of the Round Table and the Holy Grail. New York, Garland, 2000.*

Maney, Laurence J. *Looking For Arthur In All The Wrong Places.* Proceedings of The Harvard Celtic Colloquium 2004/2005.

High Kings and Pipe Dreams. Proceedings Of The Harvard Celtic Colloquium 24, 2004.

Marsden, John. *Galloglas: Hebridean and West Highland Mercenary Warrior Kindreds in Medieval Ireland.* East Linton, Scotland: Tuckwell Press, 2003.

Maynadier, Howard. *The Arthur of the English Poets.* Boston: Houghton Mifflin, 1907.

McNamara, Jo Ann, John E. Halborg, and E. Gordon Whatley, eds. *Sainted Women of the Dark Ages.* Durham, NC: Duke University Press, 1992. Medieval Scotland: Crown, Lordship and Community: Essays Presented to G.W.S Barrow. Ed. Alexander Grant and Keith J. Stringer. Edinburgh: Edinburgh University Press, 1998.

Mitchell, Kathleen, and Ian Wood. *The World of Gregory of Tours.* Boston: Brill, 2002.

Moscati, Sabatino, et al., eds. *The Celts.* New York: Rizzoli, 1991.

Moylan, Tom. *Irish Voyages and Visions: Pre-Figuring, Re-configuring Utopia.* Utopian Studies 18.3, 2007.

Müller, Friedrich Max. *Lectures on the Science of Languages.* 1862.

Murphey, G. *Two Sources in Thurneysen's Heldensage.* Ériu 15 1952.

O' Corrain & Maguire. *Irish Names, 2nd edition* Dublin. Lilliput Press, 1990.

O'Flynn, John Michael. *Generalissimos of the Western Roman Empire.* Edmonton, Alta.: University of Alberta Press, 1983.

O Maille, Tomas. *Language of the Annals OF Ulster.* Manchester University Press, 1910.

O'Rahilly, T. F. *Early Irish History and Mythology,* 1946

Orme, Nicholas. *The Saints of Cornwall.* Oxford University Press, 2000

Padel, O. J. *Arthur in Medieval Welsh Literature.* Cardiff, Wales: University of Wales Press, 2000.

Parry, Thomas D. *A History of Welsh Literature.* Trans. H. Idris Bell. Oxford: Clarendon Press, 1955.

Peden, Alison. *The Medieval Antipodes.* History Today Dec. 1995.

Petrie, George. *On the history and antiquities of Tara Hill.* Transactions of the Royal Irish Academy 18 1839.

Poole, Austin Lane. *From Domesday Book to Magna Carta, 1087-1216.* Oxford, England: Oxford University Press, 1993.

Raby, F. J. E. *A History of Christian-Latin Poetry: From the Beginnings to the Close of the Middle Ages.* Oxford: Clarendon Press, 1927.

Reeves, William. *The Life of St Columba of Hy by Adamnan.* Irish Archaeological and Celtic Society 1857.

Roberts, Brynley F. *King Arthur's Round Table: An Archaeological Investigation.* Folklore 115.1 (2004): 111+.

King Arthur: The Truth Behind the Legend. Folklore 12.22001.

Sims-Williams, Patrick. *The Celtic Inscriptions of Britain: Phonology and Chronology, c. 400-1200.* Wiley-Blackwell, 2002.

Skene, *Celtic Scotland,* Edinburgh, 1890.

Smith, B. Ed. *Britain and Ireland, 900–1300 Insular Responses to Medieval European Change.* University of Bristol 1999

Smith P. J. *Imarcaigh sund ar gach saí : An Early Modern Irish Poem on the Contemporaneous Emperors of Byzantium and the Kings and Ecclesiastics of Ireland.* University of Ulster.

Thompson, James Westfall, and Bernard J. Holm. *A History of Historical Writing.* New York: Macmillan, 1942.

Thompson, James Westfall. *The Literacy of the Laity in the Middle Ages.* New York: B. Franklin, 1963.

Thornhill, Philip. *The Origin of the Legend of King Arthur*. Mankind Quarterly 40.3 (2000): 227+.

Thurneysen, Rudolf. *A Grammar of Old Irish*. Trans. D. A. Binchy. Ed. Osborn Bergin. Dublin: Dublin Institute for Advanced Studies, 1946.

Baile Chuind Chétchathaig nach der Handschrift von Druim Snechta'. Zu irischen Handschriften und Litteraturdenkmälern. Berlin 1912.

Todd, James Henthern. *Leabhar Breathnach annso sis: The Irish version of the Historia Britonum of Nennius*. Edited with a translation and notes [from the Books of Lecan and Hy Many. Irish Archaeological SocietyDublin,1848.

Tymoczko, Maria, and Colin Ireland, eds. *Language and Tradition in Ireland: Continuities and Displacements*. Amherst, MA: University of Massachusetts Press, 2003.

Wallace-Hadrill, J. M. *Bede's Ecclesiastical History of the English People: A Historical Commentary*. Oxford: Clarendon Press, 1988.

Webster, Graham. *Rome against Caratacus: The Roman Campaigns in Britain AD 48-58*. London: Batsford, 1993.

Willis, David. *Old and Middle Welsh in The Celtic languages*. Edited by Martin Ball and Nicole Müller. Routledge 2009.

Wood, Ian. *The Merovingian Kingdoms, 450-751*. London: Longman, 1994.

Woulfe, Patrick. *Irish Names and Surnames*. Irish Genealogical Foundation; Revised edition, 1992.

Yorke, Barbara. *Kings and Kingdoms of Early Anglo-Saxon England*. London: Routledge, 1997.

Zatzikhoven, Ulrich von. *Lanzelet*. Trans. Thomas Kerth. New York: Columbia University Press, 2005.

Zeigler, Michelle, *Artur Mac Aedan of Dalriada*. Heroic Age, Issue 1, Spring/Summer 1999.

Index

Lightning Source UK Ltd.
Milton Keynes UK
UKOW051950060312

188482UK00001B/180/P